DISC GOLF:

All You Need to Know About the Game You Want to Play

Trellis Publishing, Inc.
Duluth, Minnesota

Trellis Publishing, Inc.
P.O. Box 16141
Duluth, MN 55816
800-513-0115

Disc Golf: All You Need To Know About the Game You Want To Play

© 2003, 2006 by Michael Steven Gregory

Publisher's Cataloging-in-Publication
(Provided by Quality Books, Inc.)

Gregory, Michael Steven.
    Disc golf : all you need to know about the game you want to play / Michael Steven Gregory ; illustrations by Leticia Plate.
    p.cm.
    Includes index
    LCCN 2002117777
    ISBN 1-930650-18-3

    1. Flying discs (Game)   I. Title.

GV1097.F7G74 2003   796.2
             QBI03-200088

Cover design: Foster & Foster, 800-472-3953
Book design: Gary Kruchowski, garykruchowski.efoliomn2.com
Illustrations: Leticia Plate, www.leticiaplate.com

Photos on pages 26, 27 and 29: Keri Ross Berry
Photos on pages 19, 20, 21 and 23: Discraft, Inc.

DISC GOLF:

All You Need to Know
About the Game You Want to Play

by
Michael
Steven
Gregory

TABLE OF CONTENTS
DISC GOLF: All You Need to Know About the Game You Want to Play

DEDICATION

To Nick for passing it forward, Patrick for the playmate, and Chrissie for looking fabulous on the fairway.

ACKNOWLEDGEMENTS

This book wouldn't have been written had it not been for Nicholas Berry. We met while shooting a movie in the Rockies, far away and high above our hometown of San Diego. After learning exactly where I lived, Nick got excited. "Then you must play disc golf," he concluded, pointing out that Morley Field Disc Golf Course was only two blocks from my house. He explained how he's rather new to the sport, how terrific it is, and how we have to play when we get back, and on and on. When he finished, breathless and panting the depleted air of Colorado, I asked, "What's disc golf?"

A hit off the oxygen tank later and Nick recovered enough to tell me. We made a pact to play and three weeks after I gave it a shot. Before the second round I bought my first disc. I was hooked.

My hope is that the fun and excitement of those first few rounds are very much a part of this book, as well the challenges faced following in effort to improve gameplay skills.

Many players, both pro and recreational, factor greatly into the joy of my disc golf journey. None, however, more than "Snapper" Pierson. A Disc Golf Hall of Famer, he's the man who makes Morley Field rock. Without his time, thoughtful attention, and dedication to bringing disc golf to yet another generation, we might as well be flinging flapjacks.

And to my publisher, Mary Koski, who was sensible enough to ask what that bag of discs slung over my shoulder was, thank you for your curiosity; thank you for your faith.

Enjoy!

PREFACE

Traditional club golf is fine, but here's the thing: disc golf is fun! And despite what you might think, it's as challenging as club golf in every way. Both the recreational and professional player can enjoy disc golf's exhilarating test of combining physical skill with intellectual prowess. In addition, disc golf is such a comfortably-paced outdoor sport that almost anyone can play.

In fact, despite their common verbiage, disc golf is superior to traditional golf in pretty much every way. You can play it by your lonesome or play it with your friends. You can play with your family or most any of the other estimated 300,000 other disc golfers slinging discs on nearly 1400 courses throughout the world. You don't need to spend a fortune on equipment to play disc golf; you don't need lessons to play; you don't need electric carts or half-days off work to play; you don't need to phone up ahead and schedule tee times; and maybe even best of all, you don't have to wear funny pants when you play – unless you really want to!

But don't go thinking that I'm dissin' club golf because I most definitely am not. What I am doing, however, is discing golf! Once you've played your first round, I'm sure you will too.

Enjoy!

Chapter One
WHAT IS DISC GOLF?

In the simplest terms disc golf is like traditional golf, except there's no ball, the clubs are replaced by discs and the cups by chain baskets. The objective of the game is also simple: hurl a plastic disc across a designated area and into a steel basket in the least possible throws. When finished playing a consecutive number of holes (baskets), the player with the least total throws wins.

That's it.

How we got to this refreshingly simple sport makes for a good story.

A LITTLE HISTORY

The story of disc golf starts in 1947. Two dudes, Warren Franscioni and Walter Frederick (Fred) Morrison, needed more money. Warren owned a home heating company with a partner in Southern California and Fred wanted a job. Both hailed from an aviator background - Army Air Corps, WW II. Warren served as a lieutenant in the Air Transport Service flying over India and China, and Fred was a lieutenant in fighter missions over Italy, before he got shot down and was imprisoned in Germany's infamous Stalog 13. Both were men of enterprise. Fred's dad, after all, invented the sealed automobile beam-headlamp while Warren's dad forged a name for himself in the home butane heating business elsewhere in California. So Warren hired Fred and the two dudes began working together in the home heating business.

Times were tough. Home heating in warm, sunny Southern California was hardly anybody's top priority, and putting food on the table remained a constant concern. However both men knew one thing for sure: folks everywhere liked to throw things.

Ever since the Great Depression nutty American kids enjoyed tossing metal pie tins back and forth in idle games of catch. Popularity of the game grew during the war years, as G.I.s spread it Westward from the East Coast. Now if they could just come up with a refined saucer made of a durable substance that might be marketed as a toy . . .

Bent tin quickly shredded into jagged shrapnel bits that slice meaty chunks of skin off your fingertips, and its hefty weight offered almost zero flight distance or control. So the two dudes quickly figured out that they needed a new material. See, in the aftermath of the war, plastic was coming of age. That and flying saucer sightings.

Word had gotten out about dead aliens turning up in a flying saucer that crashed in Roswell, New Mexico, in June 1947. Despite The Man trying to put the kibosh on such rumors, UFOs in the form of flying saucers became all the rave.

Warren and Fred formed a company, coined it Pipco (Partners in Plastic), got themselves a contractor to press their plastic Flyin Saucers, and began to try and sell them. Thing is, customers didn't buy them. Though they'd marvel at saucers soaring over fairgrounds during demonstrations, their sustained flight made many suspect an invisible wire was really why they stayed aloft so long. So Warren and Fred decided to just plain give the saucers away for free – with every $1 purchase of an invisible wire! But that didn't work either.

What they could do to get people enthused about piloting their very own Flyin Saucer, frankly, simply eluded the duo. That is, until Andy Capp came aboard. Andy Capp had an immensely popular comic strip at the time – *Li'l Abner* – syndicated in news-papers throughout the U.S., and he incorporated characters in it playing with Flyin Saucers. That done, Warren and Fred did what any logical, enterprising young entrepreneurs would do and included copies of the strip in their Flyin Disc packages. Big mistake, evidently, because Capp threw a wobbler, claiming the duo exceeded the provisions of their licensing contract with him, then sued Pipco for $5,000.

In those days, $5,000 was a butt-load of money. Still is. Funded out of pocket by Warren and Fred, Pipco was near bust as it was. A $5,000 payout broke the bank. Warren borrowed the needed money from his mother and mother-in-law to pay off Capp, re-enlisted with the Air Force to feed the family and was relocated to South Dakota.

Fred, meanwhile, remained in L.A. This is, like, 1953 or so. Without Warren to look over his shoulder Fred marginally redesigned the Flyin Disc, proclaimed it the "Pluto Platter" and opened up shop as American Trends to promote it.

This time it worked, but without the knowledge or involvement of Warren Franscioni. As far as Warren goes, as with so many great partnerships in history, one dude got screwed. He died 21 years later, in 1974, the year before his name was first cited as the co-inventor of what we now know to be the Frisbee. We have Frisbee historian Dr. Stancil E.D. Johnson to thank for the heads up, in his book *Frisbee: A Practitioner's Manual and Definitive Treatise*. But that's another story.

What's pertinent to disc golf is what happened in-between. Apparently, in 1955, Fred was tossing around his Pluto Platter one day in L.A. and two new dudes saw him. These two new dudes were none other than Rich Knerr and Spud Melin, who had recently founded a fledgling toy company known as Wham-O Manufacturing, based on a slingshot they'd devised for kids. Go figure.

Anyhow, they dug the Pluto Platter big time, and they saw the potential of a national sensation. They bought the license and tried to establish legitimate market demand by visiting college campuses to generate word-of-mouth. It was at Yale University that something very interesting happened. There, several students already revelled in a kind of saucer slinging sordidness (a Yale tradition since at least 1925), but with thin tin pie pans from a New England company that would go bankrupt the same year Fred was awarded his patent for a new kind of "Flying Toy,"

1958. In a riff off traditional golf's "Fore!" warning, students yelped the company's name, plainly embossed on the pans, whenever slinging them skyward and in harm's way. The name of that ill-fortunate bakery, of course? That's right, the one and only Frisbie Baking Company of Bridgeport, Connecticut.

A slight tweak of the spelling by Wham-O and the name stuck for good. The Pluto Platter was dead – long live the "Frisbee!"

Flash forward to 1964. The Beatles invade America, Elvis lives, Day-Glo is coming, the Hula Hoop shimmies around gyrating waistlines of giddy citizens everywhere, and the Frisbee, well, the Frisbee still hasn't quite taken off (pun intended).

But see, there's this other guy in the California water heating business, a savvy marketing maven cum inventor, who's got a hankering for a new challenge in his otherwise successful professional life. He's come up with a new kind of hydrofoil water ski, tucks it under his arm, and goes knocking on the door of Wham-O, hoping for a sale. Wham-O, of course, just also happens to manufacture the Hoola Hoop.

Now legend has it (legend which happens to be true) that Wham-O wasn't particularly interested in the inventor's water ski, but was intrigued by his brash offer to quit the high-paying job he held as vice president/general manager of the water heater company to work for free for three months as head of the research & development (marketing) department. If Wham-O liked what he came up with after the three-month trial period, he would be paid retroactively. As it stood, Wham-O was losing thousands of dollars a month on useless Hula Hoop tubing storage alone, so new ideas were welcome.

The inventor went to work on his first idea: let's take all that useless Hula Hoop plastic sitting in a costly warehouse and sell it to a meltdown company.

This got Wham-O's attention and saved them a fortune. Within his three-month trial period the inventor then devised his own vision of a flying saucer and filed a patent. He un-earthed Wham-O's Pluto Platter mold and pressed a test version, added some sparkle – in this case a gold foil label and black-painted ring – labelled it a "Pro" model and shot a TV commercial.

Oh, and also in those first three months of trial employment, the inventor took a gob of synthetic rubber developed by the tire industry and invented the Super Ball! In very short order both the Frisbee and the Super Ball became two of the top ten fads in the world.

Needless to say the inventor got the job, his backpay, plus $10 for valuable consideration from Wham-O. That inventor's name was "Steady" Ed Headrick, undisputed Father of the modern Frisbee.

And that's just the beginning of what evolutionary enterprise would ultimately deliver to us all as the game of disc golf. It took a few years weaning, what with Steady Ed forming an organization to first bolster the legitimacy of Frisbee to saucer enthusiasts worldwide (the International Frisbee Association), then launching a competitive event (the Junior Frisbee Championships) that would evolve into a major annual affair staged at the Rose Bowl (the World Frisbee Championships), but by the time he left Wham-O in 1975, Steady Ed still had not yet truly discovered the game he felt would resonate beyond the playful toy perception of the masses or free-styling niche players. Until, at least by his own admission, he had "an amazing revelation."

Story goes that Steady Ed and his friends often played Frisbee in the park, "throwing at trees, drinking fountains, open car windows and the occasional coed." IFA and champion Frisbeer Dan Roddick had persuaded a reluctant Steady Ed to include a similar Frisbee golf game in his Wham-O-sponsored events. The chained ground targets that were used in this earliest incarnation of disc golf sparked Steady Ed's imagination to invent something new. It took 56 attempts to realize, but when he was finished, he'd created something brilliant - a contraption of such solidly simple singularity, such glimmering gorgeousness, that it would change everything. His revelation? The elevated steel chain basket target.

Despite Steady Ed's marketing efforts and his creation of the Professional Disc Golfers Association (some 12,000 members strong by 2002) and, later the Recreational Disc Golfers Association, in those early days disc golf still remained nothing more than a grassroots pastime played with traditional Frisbees by aging hippies and their offspring. Enter Jan Sobel.

See, until 1983 disc golf really was still nothing more than golf played with traditional Frisbees intended to be tossed and caught. But Frisbees performed poorly in the wind, they were difficult to control, and they were just plain hard to throw well for almost everybody. Jan was ready for a change. What he aimed to do was engineer a disc specifically geared to the demands of the game. He made his disc flatter, heavier, and smaller. He called it a Puppy. It was an immediate hit with those who were already taking the game seriously, and ultimately the Puppy became the prototype from which many others were built. A new era of disc golf had been ushered in and its evolution escalated.

Like many players at the time, World Frisbee Distance Champion Dave Dunipace also thought it time for a change. In his words, "I wanted to make the sport more dynamic by introducing drivers to the game that basically had a putter at best."

Dave went to Harold Duvall, then PDGA Champion, with his idea for a disc designed specifically for the sport. Harold and his brother, Charlie, said they'd fund it, and their friend Tim Selinske would run the business and handle customers face-to-face at their first shop. The Four Discateers picked up Steady Ed's fizzling torch, improved upon Jan's disc design approach, and set out with a mission: let's change the counterculture Frisbee-faction perception of the game into that of a sport worthy of professional-level merit.

Of course, a professional sport requires tools uniquely designed to meet the challenges of professional gameplay. So in short order their company ditched the Frisbee, created disc categories and, in rapid succession, invented a series of bevel-edged, high performance, non-catch, wind sheering discs geared to perform specific functions within each category. They marketed disc golf aggressively and helped make it mainstream by introducing heavy duty pro-model baskets and adding professional course design to the equation.

Other companies and countless individuals equally passionate about the sport contributed to the groundswell of support for disc golf. Course growth in the U.S. almost tripled from 400 to nearly 1200 courses in only six years, and today – more than two decades after its inauspicious debut – disc golf continues to make history. Now, simply by playing disc golf, you're a part of that history!

Chapter Two
WHAT YOU WANT TO KNOW: THE BASICS

What you want to do right now is go throw some discs – and you should – just as soon as you're finished reviewing some basics. In fact, think of this book as you might an instruction manual for a VCR. It should be the little book you reach for only after you've been hosed trying to figure everything out for yourself. This is your DGP (Disc Golf Player's) manual. Read this chapter, go throw a round or two, and when you have the time and inclination, come on back and delve deeper into the many ways you might improve your game and increase your enjoyment.

This book will be here when you're ready, so let's get on with it.

HOW TO PLAY

Disc golf is played with plastic discs specially crafted for the sport. Available in a variety of shapes and weights, they're generally categorized as drivers, approach discs and putters.

The courses on which disc golf is played also vary, both in terrain and number of holes available. The standard game is 18 holes, which takes roughly an hour to play, although there are many courses that have only nine holes or even fewer. Each hole consists of a tee pad or teeing area, a fairway, and a designated target. The standard target is an elevated chain pinbasket commonly referred to as the "hole," or "basket" or "pin" (Figure 2.1).

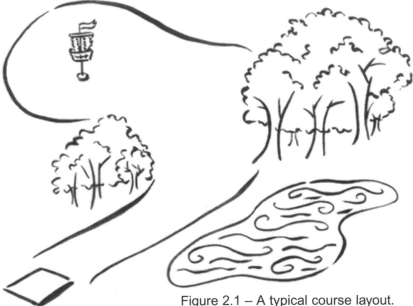

Figure 2.1 – A typical course layout.

The game is played by throwing your disc toward the hole from a tee pad and then landing the disc in the basket in the fewest throws. As each player progresses down the fairway, s/he must throw each consecutive shot from the exact spot where the previous throw landed. This spot is known as the "lie." When your disc finally lands in the basket, the hole is completed and you and the other players proceed to the next hole.

Once all the holes have been played, total the number of throws each player took (which has been consistently noted on the crumpled scoresheet in your pocket) and determine who threw the least number of times. The player with the lowest score wins.

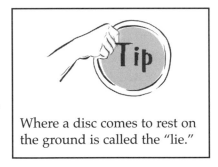

Where a disc comes to rest on the ground is called the "lie."

Nifty thing about disc golf, though, is that you don't necessarily have to play against other players to get the juices flowing. While it's fun to hang out and play together, simply by playing at all you're competing against par – par for each hole, par for the course and, ultimately, the lowest figure that you've ever played on these holes. If beating your best score doesn't spike your gameplay gumption, then where's the fun in trampling the scores of your friends?

WHAT IS PAR?

In case you are unfamiliar with the term, "par" is the average number of throws a practiced player is expected to make in order to complete a course. Every hole has a predetermined par. While one hole might be a par three – meaning the average number of throws it takes to get a disc into the basket is no more than three – and another four, once you add them all together, what you get is the total figure that is considered par for the course. As with so many things in life we consider being "par for the course," so it is with disc golf, except not even close!

In fact, at least on the more challenging courses, just getting within 20 throws above par (on an 18 hole course) is something to feel good about your first time around. And should you some-how actually equal course par then – Dude! – crack open the cheese puffs because you've managed to play with a skill equivalent to what's considered "aver-age" for the practiced player. Score underneath course par? Well, jot it down and start strumming the six-string 'cause that's truly something to sing about. The greater the number under par you shoot, the greater the disc slinging superstar you are.

Now whether it's the signature steel-chained baskets which qualify a course as being a professional-worthy disc golf play-ing field (Figure 2.2) or some other fixed target, consistently reaching each and every hole within par will ultimately remain your number one objective.

Figure 2.2 – The standard pin basket, or "hole."

EQUIPMENT AND SUPPLIES

As with most sports, there are accessaries you can buy that will facilitate game enjoyment. All you really need, however, are discs, and since the discs themselves play such pivotal a role, let's start by taking a closer look at them.

DISCS

There are lots of discs available to the disc golf player, and it seems everybody has an opinion about which ones are best for whom. It can get mighty confusing, because most opinions are correct. Each disc, when used skillfully, has a distinct role in the game.

• Drivers

A driver is designed to traverse the greatest distance from any given throw (Figure 2.3a). Slightly flatter than other discs, drivers are specifically engineered to slice through the air with the least amount of wind resistance to extend their flight. Usually it is the first disc you'll throw from each tee pad.

Figure 2.3a – Driver, Discraft Wasp

• Approach Discs

Similar in design to drivers, "approach" or "mid-range" discs are typically distinguished by a more rounded edge (Figure 2.3b), so they tend not to travel as far or skip as much as a precisely thrown driver. You'll use them most often when you are throwing midway between the tee pad and the basket, as you begin to near (or approach) the putting zone of the hole.

Figure 2.3b – Approach Disc, Discraft Wildcat

20

If you're packing a limited arsenal, carry an approach disc that can also serve you well when used as a driver.

• **Putters**

The disc that will make or break every hole of your game is the "put-ter" (Figure 2.3c). Unlike drivers and approach discs, which share similar characteristics and can be used interchangeably by many play-ers, the putter is geared for one thing only: chain-slamming accuracy when thrown, say, within ten yards of the basket. Distinguished by a very round, sometimes even right-angled edge and thick lip, your put-ting disc, (when skillfully used) can salvage your score as well as your oclf-esteem.

Figure 2.3c - Putter, Discraft Challenger

If you carry only two discs onto the course, definitely make one a putter.

• **Markers (or mini-discs)**

This is a miniature version of a regular playing disc, measur-ing about four inches in diameter. Aside from being handy for a quick game of dinky-disc golf, they serve a valid purpose in marking the spot where a disc has landed (the "lie"), since this is the spot from where you will throw next.

By no means mandatory except in earnestly competitive or profes-sional play, markers are nice to have if for no other reason than to avoid stepping on a disc and dam-aging it. Plus, you'll look like a PDGA player when you're using one and you'll impress everybody around you.

Don't step on your discs! They become warped and we call them tacos!

• **Renting Discs**

If you're fortunate enough to be playing on a course that has a pro shop, chances are they'll have discs available to rent for only a buck or two a day. One benefit of renting discs is that they're usually pretty worn in. Though made of plastic, a disc's performance characteristics can change dramatically over the long haul of constant gameplay. "Test driving" rental discs can provide you valuable insight into how a given brand or model will perform long after that molten plastic showroom gleam has faded, saving you the expense and frustration of buying discs you won't ever use or that don't fit your throwing style.

• **Buying Discs**

Discs are very affordable, ranging in price from about $8 to $20 each. You can buy them online and at most well-stocked sporting goods stores. The real consideration for purchase isn't so much the monetary cost of any given disc, but the value the disc will ultimately have to you in your expanding throwing reper- toire. Once you buy a disc and discover it doesn't do what you want, unless you're able to adapt your throw to compensate (which often is the problem to begin with), you wind up with a disc that you can't return and that you'll rarely use.

It never hurts to have an extra disc or two lying around for friends to use, or just to have on hand in case one of your favorite discs gets treed or lost. Do remember to write your name and phone number inside with a permanent marker as soon as you buy a disc. On more than a few occasions I've found spanking new discs stuck in a tree or under a bush some- where and had no way to return them to the rightful owner. Guess what? They're mine now!

DISC BAG

There's an ample assortment of disc golf bags on the market. Made of canvas or synthetic material and featuring a shoulder strap and maybe a drink holder, what distinguishes one from the next is basically disc capacity and extra compartments, used for stashing things like scoresheets, pencils, car keys, etc. (Figure 2.4). The average style can hold around a dozen discs comfort- ably for easy retrieval, while some professional-line models fea- ture accordion-style dividers and larger storage pouches that carry up to 24 discs or more. With disc golf bag prices ranging from $15 to $85, practicality of design should be the only determining factor for choosing the bag that's right for you. Why? Because although it'd be nice to have a jumbo bag full of twentysomething discs, like many touring pros use, realistically speaking you're going to find yourself playing with the same three or four discs almost all the time.

Figure 2.4 – Bags for carrying discs and other items.

Instead of worrying about lugging around a weighty, dizzying variety of discs that you won't ever use, carry only those few that you know work best in the situations you moot frequently encounter. Base your bag choice on things like extra pockets for your stuff, internal framing to prevent the bag from toppling over every time you set it down to throw, zipper and Velcro-sealing pouches, adjustable dividers, and just plain, simple comfort.

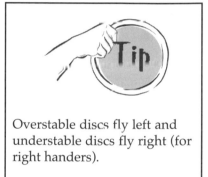

Overstable discs fly left and understable discs fly right (for right handers).

TOWELS

Having a towel handy makes your life a little easier on any disc golf course. Strap it to your bag so you can wipe your discs off when you need to because, believe me, you will need to.

What happens is you're lobbing discs along and each time they touch down they either get wet and muddy from the recent sprinklers or rainfall, or they get all dusty and grubby from the dirt and tree trunks they bite chunks out of. Either way,

Very few courses have on-site pro shops to rent or buy discs and supplies.

all that slickness and grit that forms along the lip and outer surface of your disk becomes a tactile intrusion interfering with your concentration and disrupting your throws. Why worry about it? Just do yourself a favor and carry a towel. If you don't want to buy a proper disc golf towel, then at least carry a bar towel or hand towel so you can focus on your game without spoiling your t-shirt.

CLOTHING

Disc golf is a casual game, so courses have no restrictions on dress. Common sense and comfort are really the only consideration when deciding what to wear when you play.

• Tops and bottoms

Given that the sport is played outside and involves plenty of walking and upper body movement, roomy shorts or pants and t-shirts, polo shirts, or tank tops which allow freedom of movement are your best bets on the course. Clothing made of natural fabrics will best help prevent your body from overheating. Do keep in mind the value of dressing in layers. While you might start a round feeling a bit chilly, there's sufficient body movement in disc golf to generate enough heat to get uncomfortably warm very quickly. It's a good idea to always be prepared for excess heat, regardless of the weather; be able to shed a layer so your body can breathe.

• Shoes

Comfortable sneakers or some other lightweight closed-toe shoe is generally good for any disc golf course. Given the amount of walking, as well the terrain variations you tend to find on courses, shoes that breathe and provide arch and lateral support are best; those with a good tread to reduce slipping when you throw or need to climb a tree are also a major plus.

MISCELLANEOUS SUPPLIES

Scoresheets are available free of charge at almost any disc golf course with a pro shop, and even a few without. Obviously, make sure you carry along a pencil to write with, again free at most on-site pro shops.

Other supplies that are handy to have include a permanent

marker, nail clipper and sandpaper. The permanent marker is simply to write your name and phone number inside any new disc you buy. If you're buying discs from the course pro shop, chances are they have a marker available specifically for this purpose.

Nail clippers and sandpaper are nice to have to smooth out the jagged edges that sometimes result when a disc dings a tree trunk, rock or other hard surface. The nail clipper is used to cut the torn shard of plastic that sticks out from the disc's edge. The sandpaper is used to smooth the gouge left behind.

FIRST AID AND HYDRATION

With almost any physical activity, there is inevitably some risk of injury. It's no different when playing disc golf. From minor scrapes suffered slipping in mud or tripping over stones to more serious incidents, it's good to be prepared. I once scratched the cornea of my eyeball so severely with a tree branch some 20 feet off the ground, that I couldn't see through the blinding white pain and tears to shimmy my way back down safely. It's always wise to have a little first aid kit in your bag, or at least a Band-Aid or two and some rubbing alcohol. In my case, morphine would have been welcomed.

One last thing that can not be emphacized enough: water. The body gets thirsty, especially outside and when in motion. Do yourself a favor and replenish it often.

Chapter Three
YOUR FIRST 18 HOLES

You've got your gear. You've got the gumption. Let's get your first game in.

DRIVE OFF THE TEE

Figure 3.1 – The hole as seen from the pad.

You stand poised on the tee pad of hole one, driver in hand. A sign marks the spot where the basket lays ahead. You squint into the distance but don't see it at first. Then, just beyond the bramble, slightly to the right – There! – in the copse of trees which form a low canopy of spidery branches overhead, you see the basket (Figure 3.1). Much closer than you thought, really. The sign says par three. How hard can it be?

You grip the disc tight, curl your arm back and let it rip. The disc goes flying up high and away. Hopeful, you catch your breath and watch, settling back on your heels as your stomach starts to sink. Ever so quickly, it seems, the disc careens away in the opposite direction of the basket, plopping down half as far as you thought it might.

You suck – welcome to disc golf!

Figure 3.2 – The hole as seen from the lie.

THROW FROM THE LIE

From the spot where your first throw landed, you can see the basket more clearly (Figure 3.2). You pick up your disc and prepare to throw again, careful not to step past where it came to rest. Your arm's a little looser now, and the distant target is plainly in sight. With a quick

Always yell "Fore!" if there's a possibility of striking another player with a disc in flight.

fling, you set your disc sailing once more.

You yell "Fore!" to alert unsuspecting players a disc is coming in hot. Then you watch powerlessly as it banks hard to one side and cuts into the treeline. When it sticks to the upper branches you can't believe your bad luck. Suddenly, gravity starts working and tugs at the disc. A glimmer of good fortune, you think, when earthward it topples, but not long enough, my friend; the disc does not fall far enough.

Do not use discs to try and knock other discs out of trees, or you'll have more than one disc stuck in a tree.

If gravity doesn't do the job, you'll find yourself standing under a disc out of reach – you've been treed. Of course, not knowing that the cardinal sin of disc golf is to throw a disc into a tree to knock another disc down, you do just that – you throw another disc up at the first, only to lodge it equally inextricably in the branches, and out of reach. Now you've got two discs stuck in a tree!

Fortunately, since there are no other players waiting behind you (in which case you'd demonstrate good course etiquette and invite them to "throw through"), you find a couple of rocks and in short order knock the discs out of the tree to resume play. The current lie is the place directly beneath where your first disc got stuck (Figure 3.3).

"Tree whackers" are what many new players are known as by those who've been playing awhile!

Had you not gotten stuck, this would be your third throw, but since the disc was treed it counts as a stroke against you. What you're most focused on now is simply getting within putting range of the basket. This was only a par three hole, right? And you're now on what, with the penalty, throw four?

Not that there's anything wrong with that. We're here to have fun, right? Just toss some discs in the sun and have a few laughs! Right?

What's important is that you're primed and you want to throw, so that's what you do. Mindful of the wiry branches hanging low overhead, this time you throw your disc level and it dings a tree trunk and kicks back toward the pin, actually touching down within putting distance of the basket. Hey, whenever it works to your benefit, we call that "tree love." The scoresheet doesn't care.

Figure 3.3 – The lie for a treed disc.

Though maybe your disc didn't go as far as you'd hoped, you're still in the game. Grateful for the break, you go to the lie and cizo up the shot which will define your very first putt.

PUTT

Hunched no more than five, maybe six yards away from the hole, you break out your putter disc. Short distance accuracy is all we're talking about here. The only thing you're wanting to do is sling some bad boy plastic smack into some dumb dangling chain.

You eyeball the basket, putter firmly fingered, you inhale. You fling. You watch. You breathe. And you blow it big time, the disc drifts lazily past the basket, not even coming close.

What is up with that? At this point sheer spite kicks in and you stomp over to the putter, snatch it up from the ground and just lob it – CHING! – straight into the basket. Congratulations, you've completed your first hole.

You yell "Clear!" to those waiting back at the tee pad and traipse over to hole two.

HOW TO SCORE

Figure 3.4 shows the basic elements necessary to keep score. Simply write down the number of throws each player makes to complete a hole, then total the numbers after you've completed the round.

Counting the added penalty stroke to make for a triple bogey, you just scored a whopping six on hole one. A par three hole.

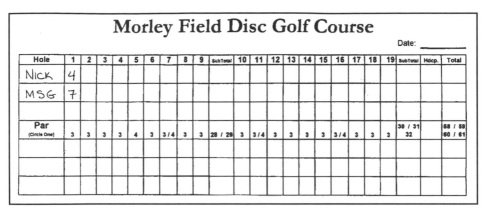

Figure 3.4 – Standard score sheet.

WHO THROWS FIRST NEXT

Whoever threw the least number of times on the previous hole gets to go first on the next. And now that you're there you get to do it all over again. Big difference, however, is this time you're ready; you got it all worked out. You get it. I mean, there's only so many holes on a course. How hard could it be?

YOU'RE READY

And that's all there is to it. You now know everything you need to know to play disc golf, except for all the other stuff you'll really want to know to improve your skills. Go play and have fun.

Chapter Four
WHAT YOU NEED TO KNOW: BEYOND THE BASICS

Figure 4.1 – Frisbees are thrown to be caught.

Having now played a round or three, you have to admit you're more than a little surprised at how much fun the game is. That's the natural response to playing disc golf for the first time. Now the question is, "How do I play better?"

UNLEARNING WHAT YOU'VE LEARNED

Although one might assume the differences between throwing disc golf discs and throwing Frisbees would be negligible, in reality the two have little in common. In fact, for the newly committed disc golfer, the biggest obstacle to improving skills is simply unlearning the way we threw Frisbees in our youth. The absolute very first thing you need to remember about disc golf then, is this:

It ain't Frisbee golf!

Frisbees, the Wham-O! brand plastic platters we tossed around as kids, are not only lighter in weight and shaped differently than the plastic platters used by disc golfers, but also, and most importantly, their purpose for existing is entirely different. Both Zen and aerodynamically speaking, we don't even want to go there yet!

We threw Frisbees as kids primarily for somebody to catch. To that end we threw them high so they'd float long enough to allow one of our playmates to maneuver underneath and snatch them out of the sky (Figure 4.1). No matter where you threw a Frisbee, if someone didn't have a shot at nabbing it you could at the very least rely on your dog to do so. That's what Frisbee is about – you toss one up, somebody (or some canine-critter) goes to catch it on the way down.

It's different with disc golf. In disc golf we throw at an immobile target a hundred to several hundred feet away, typically a small basket of galvanized steel chains suspended on a pole some 27 inches off the ground. We must throw our discs low, not only to exert control over their trajectory, but also to avoid those elements which inevitably conspire to impede their intended flight path (Figure 4.2). Accuracy and distance are the principle objectives when throwing our discs. The ultimate goal is to reach the

Figure 4.2 – Disc golf discs are thrown at a fixed target.

basket and deliver to our ears that singularly resonant CHING! of chain smashing satisfaction that signals our success.

The level of controlled accuracy achieved will be dependent on how effectively you disassociate the familiar physical motion inherent to flinging Frisbees from that of throwing disc golf discs.

I use the word "fling" in reference to Frisbees specifically because this distinction cannot be over-emphasized.

When you're readying to fling a Frisbee, what you typically do is stand with it tucked close to your ribs, wrist bent inward, forearm almost touching plastic, elbow crooked at about 45 degrees to form a sort of "J" shape from shoulder to fingers (Figure 4.3). The action used to fling a Frisbee comes from the elbow pulling down as it extends, wrist flicking upward before you release with a back-hand swing. Consequently, what with so little momentum brought to bare from the rest of your body, the Frisbee is propelled only by the strength of

Figure 4.3 – The "J" shape used to throw a Frisbee.

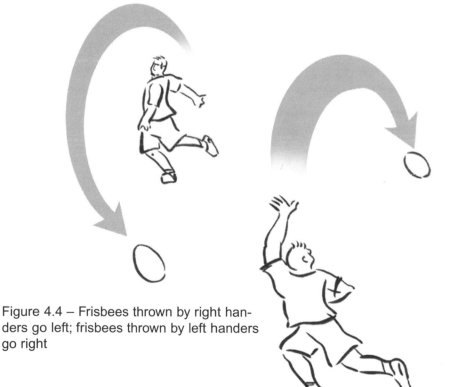

Figure 4.4 – Frisbees thrown by right handers go left; frisbees thrown by left handers go right

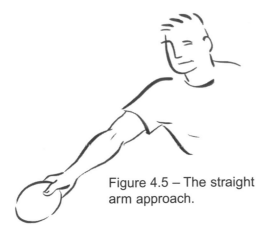

Figure 4.5 – The straight arm approach.

your arm until it runs out of juice and glides inevitably in the opposite direction of whichever hand was used to throw it – right handers go left; left handers go right (Figure 4.4).

When launching disc golf discs, at least with drives and long approach shots, forget about crooking your elbow; forget about flicking your wrist; try to use your whole body and its momentum. Try to break any bad Frisbee throwing habits. While I address proper disc driving technique at length in Chapter Eight, for now you should endeavor to keep your arm relatively straight, with your wrist staying in line with your forearm (Figure 4.5).

Grip figures heavily into this new-way-of-throwing equation. With Frisbees, your hold of the platter tends to be rather loose and casual. With disc golf discs, your grip should be tight, much like a fist, with the edge of the disc clenched firmly in between your throwing hand's thumb and index finger (Figure 4.6).

Figure 4.6 - Disc golf grip.

Except maybe the pinky (depending on what works best for you), all your other digits should also be curled tightly under the disc, tips pressed hard against the inner lip of the disc's edge.

When you throw – again we're talking primarily drives and approach here – your arm should be fairly straight. Allow the weight of your body's rotation to bolster the momentum of your shoulder and propel the disc. Step into the drive, rotate your body, follow through with your arm and release the disc with a snap of your index finger (Figure 4.7). Your discs will travel farther.

Figure 4.7 – Technique for a common drive.

Trying to remember all these things when you're first starting out and standing on the pad ain't easy. Not only is the whole approach to throwing fundamentally unlike throwing Frisbees, but throwing can also be physically uncomfortable. If it's too much to deal with (which is the case for most everybody), break it apart and focus on one aspect of your drive at a time. Concentrate on your grip, for example, then once you've mastered that, move on to the next step. When you start getting used to putting all the separate elements together successfully – training your arm, your feet and your release to work with seamless fluidity – I promise you'll begin to notice a marked improvement in your gameplay.

Tip

Remember to completely follow through with your arm, don't lock up mid-swing!

One other key element to improving your drive is to watch others who toss well. Watch their stance. Watch how they grip their discs, watch how they release, and learn. And never hesitate to ask for advice. While what works for one player might not necessarily work for you, never pass up the opportunity to glean that one morsel of insight from another player that may substantially improve your game performance.

By moving beyond these basic adjustments and fine-tuning your repertoire of throwing techniques, you'll be busting par in no time.

BEYOND THE BASICS

Now that you know what separates throwing Frisbees from throwing disc golf discs, as well as how to rethink your approach to better exploit those differences, let's look at the more subtle contrasts between the discs you'll be using.

Backhand throwing right handers' discs will naturally want to fade left; left handers' discs will naturally want to fade right.

UNDERSTANDING DISC STABILITY

Even sober, on close inspection the superficial characteristics that distinguish one disc from another can be so infinitesimal as to make you doubt whether any relevant difference exists between them at all. Don't let this fool you. Difference there is. Big time.

Shape, weight distribution, and material composition all factor into how a disc will ultimately perform in flight. Regardless of your throwing

Figure 4.8 – Overstable, stable and understable disc flight patterns.

prowess, the disc itself will dictate the control with which you wield it. Design intent and engineering assures the disc will go a certain way, with or without you. There are three divisions of disc performance definition: stable, overstable and understable (Figure 4.8), and understanding disc behavior is half the battle of mastering your throws.

STABLE DISCS

A stable disc naturally flies fairly straight when thrown level. As it slows it breaks neither left nor right. This type of disc will maintain a relatively straight line when released properly.

OVERSTABLE DISCS

A disc which naturally flies in the opposite direction of its rotation-when it's thown, is regarded as an overstable disc. For a right hander, the disc will fade left.

Throwing a disc accurately is more important than throwing a disc far. Stay away from understable distance discs if you can't control them, and use stable discs you can keep on the fairway.

UNDERSTABLE DISCS

A disc which naturally flies in the same direction as its rotation as it slows, when thrown level, is regarded as an understable disc. For a right hander, the disc will fade to the right, opposite the direction of an overstable disc.

FINDING THE BEST DISCS

There are so many discs on the market today, it can get very confusing (not to mention expensive) trying to figure out which ones to buy. The brand disc cheat chart (Appendix A) provides a reasonably accurate summary of what to expect from some of the most popular models currently available. New models are introduced often, so never hesitate to ask other players which discs they're using and how the discs work for them.

SUMMARY

So that's basically it. No way, you say. That's it? That's all I need to know to move past being a newbie tree-whacker to a finely-tuned disc tosser? Just don't throw like when you're throwing catch-Frisbee and figure out which discs fly what direction?

Well, yes and no. It's the first place to start in order to better understand the things we'll discuss in the following chapters. But those things, like all things that warrant a commitment and investment of time in pursuit of some personal gratification, are best addressed one toss at a time.

Chapter Five
THROWING TECHNIQUES

Sometimes there's more than one way to approach a hole. Whether worm burning down a slopin' dog-leg fairway in the wind, or drilling straight through some chaparral alley, or chucking blind up a forested ravine, expanding your available throwing options is instrumental to good gameplay. The key to doing so is having a variety of throws at your disposal that you can rely on when you need them.

While the disc you elect to use is an important factor in the outcome of most throws (refer to Appendix A's disc cheat sheet), ultimately it's the manner in which you throw the disc that dictates overall performance. What follows are the throws you'll want in your repertoire. Each throw is comprised of four distinct parts:

Grip - How you hold the disc.

Stance - The placement of your feet as you begin the throw.

Windup - The physical motion of your body as it feeds the disc to its release point.

Release - The position of your wrist, hand and fingers when releasing the disc.

Do also consider focus as a fundamental part of your overall technique. Focus is knowing prior to release not only where you want the disc to land, but the necessary adjustments that must be made to your grip and release to get it there.

THROWING BACKHAND

The backhand is where it all starts. Most of us are inherently drawn to the backhand, ever since first flinging Frisbees on the front lawn. Basically, it's throwing the disc across your chest with the back of your hand leading the way.

Grip

With the backhand throw, make a fist and slip the disc's edge into it.

Start by pressing the rim of your driver or approach disc solidly across the inner fold of the palm. Extend your thumb along the top edge of the disc, curl at least three fingers directly underneath, pressing their tips firmly against the disc's inner lip. Apply most of the pressure to your thumb and index finger tip (Figure 5.1).

Now jerk your wrist a few times to ensure the disc doesn't waffle, but stays firmly in place. Its top plane should be parallel to your forearm, its nearest edge (maybe an inch's worth max), touching your inner wrist squarely in the middle. If the outer edge of the disc sags in your grip you're holding it too loosely. Tighten up.

Figure 5.1 – Backhand grip.

Stance

With the backhand throw there's a lot of latitude on initial stance (and the windup which follows) because you'll be using it in a variety of situations. Off the pad you are seeking both accuracy and distance. On approach it is less about distance and more about accuracy.

Given that three of the following chapters are devoted in their entirety to improving specific aspects of your gameplay technique using the standard backhand throw – your putt (Chapter Six), your approach (Chapter Seven) and your drive (Chapter

Eight) – we'll address only the basic distinctions of the stance. Fancy footwork can wait.

Draw in your mind a straight line leading from you to the basket. Plant your feet on the line with the foot opposite your throwing arm being the one farthest from the hole, about 2 ft. behind the other. With feet and shoulders along the same imaginary line, lift your throwing arm towards the hole, without bending your elbow.

You are now turned at a 90 degree angle away from the hole, your feet and shoulders positioned straight along the imaginary

Figure 5.2 – Backhand stance.

line leading to the basket. This is the approximate stance you want to be in when you release your disc (Figure 5.2), except your eyes should be focused on where you want the disc to be propelled upon release (more on that later).

Windup

There are several ways to step into, or windup, your backhand throw. Simply relying on arm strength won't cut it. In order to achieve distance (and control) you must bring the momentum of your entire body to bear in the moments just before releasing the disc.

Think of a steel coil being wound so tight it's quivering with kinetic energy just busting to break loose. Think of the instant all that energy can no longer be contained and – SPRANG! – the coil unleashes. Well, that's the same thinking you should put into your windup.

Your windup, the physical steps you take as you rotate your body and funnel its energy from your feet to your fingers at the precise moment of release, will launch your disc farther than mere muscle can ever manage.

Release

How you want your disc to perform will dictate the final position of your wrist, hand, and fingers when releasing a backhand throw. "Backhand" is merely the catchall phrase for a throwing technique, not the actual throw itself. Some people gravitate to a "sidearm" throwing technique, for instance, because it's more natural for them.

THROWING SIDEARM

The sidearm, like the backhand, is another catchall term for a style of throwing. In this case the disc is slung from the side of the body, its path led by the palm of the throwing hand (Figure 5.3).

The most important distinction of the sidearm is that the disc's flight trajectory (when thrown relatively level) will almost always be opposite that of a backhand. Right handers throwing backhand will find their discs

Figure 5.3 – Sidearm throw.

really wanting to travel to the left, and left handers will find their discs wanting to go right. Throwing sidearm makes the discs go the opposite direction. That is, an overstable disc that would naturally fade left for a right-handed backhander will now fade right as a result of a sidearm throw. It's good to remember this when confronted with a shot you absolutely must arc to the side of your throwing arm.

Grip

For a sidearm throw the disc is basically held level with your palm and wrist facing up, one or two fingers extended underneath the disc, thumb crossing the top plane and the disc edge tucked into its crook. But as with most things in disc golf, the best grip for one player may not be what's best for another – and the sidearm grip definitely proves that.

Figure 5.1   Sidearm grip.

Some players prefer to extend both the middle and pointer fingers underneath the disc in a kind of "peace sign" fashion. The pad of their index finger is pressed firmly against the inner lip of the disc while the pointer extends toward the middle in order to level it out and keep it from wobbling during the windup (Figure 5.4).

Figure 5.5 – Sidearm grip option.

Others prefer to curl only the pointer finger tight against the inner lip with the thumb placed along the top surface edge above it, clenching all other fingers into the palm (Figure 5.5).

I prefer the "peace sign" method of sidearm grip for a long distance throw. I feel it gives me greater control over the disc's stability in my hand before it's released.

Whichever of these methods ultimately works best for you (maybe it'll even be some weird combination of the two), the only thing to remember is that what works best for you is what works best, period. Don't let anybody tell you differently!

Stance

Now stance for the sidearm throw can be a funny thing, and not pretty. In order to keep the disc parallel to the ground you have to hunch sideways, which is not an entirely comfortable thing on your ribcage. And forget the imaginary line that connects you to the distant basket. With the sidearm you're facing the basket for the entire duration of windup, release and follow-through. Essentially, you end up walking the line toward the hole before release.

Also, unlike the backhand, momentum with the sidearm is derived mostly from arm movement and wrist action. Generally speaking there's not a lot of body movement involved in the sidearm, just a few short footsteps and with a quick flick of the wrist, the disc snaps off your finger.

Windup

Walking the imaginary line that binds you to the basket is really what's behind the sidearm, at least for distance. With the sidearm, holding your disc firm and level – or tipped steeply in the direction of a sharp flight path – is key. Take a step or two toward your release point, which in this case will be one side or the other of your imaginary line, and snap the disc off your finger.

Considering the lack of windup, you might suspect that the sidearm isn't really a viable option for throwing long distance shots, but let me tell you, I've seen many players simply walk up to the pad, flick a sidearm and send a disc farther than some of the more powerful long-distance backhanders. Just play with it and see what you think.

Release

The secret to throwing a good, long distance sidearm is a smooth flick of the wrist and snap of the disc off your finger tip. Your hand should release palm up, primary finger extended and stinging from the ferocity of the snap.

And, baby, it's always about the "snap"!

THROWING OVERHAND

An overhand throw (often called a toma-hawk) is used to get yourself out of a tricky situation. For the most part it's chucking the disc hard and high to cut through, sometimes over, whatever obstacles are impeding a clean flight path to the basket. Heavily wood-ed terrain often presents the need to have a reliable overhand throw.

Grip
Make a little pistol with your throwing hand – the "bang, bang" kind we did as kids – and set the edge of the disc into the fleshy bit between the thumb and pointer finger. With the disc's top plane facing your body, pinch

Figure 5.6 – Overhand throw.

pointer and thumb together along its edge to hold it firmly in place. Now raise the disc nearly vertical to the ground (Figure 5.6).

This is your basic tomahawk grip, but as with many grips there are variations which may have good results. For instance, placing not one but two fingers inside the disc will ensure it trav-els left to right. Flipping the disc so that the top faces away from the body and hooking the thumb inside will get the disc to travel right to left. And if thrown hard enough, the disc will even man-age to roll a full 360 degrees and fly right side up.

Stance
Stand on the imaginary line between you and the basket, the foot of your throwing arm side about two feet behind the other. Lean back and place the bulk of your weight on the back foot, bending your knees slightly. Now raise the disk close to your head, maybe six inches behind your ear, and relax your wrist.

Windup
Depending on the predicament you're in, windup may or may not involve any real footwork to speak of. Off the tee pad you have plenty of room to step into the throw and use your body's

momentum to sling a disc hard overhead. Out in the bushes it's unlikely you'll have that kind of space, so you will have to rely on form and sheer shoulder power to chuck the disc.

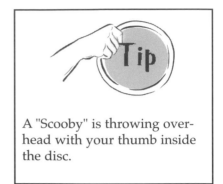

A "Scooby" is throwing over-head with your thumb inside the disc.

Ideally you will add to the momentum of the throw from a slight spring of your throwing side foot, on which most of your weight is placed.

Release

A sharp snap has little to do with the tomahawk. Less snap, more arm and more precision is the order of the day. Let the disc roll forward off your finger(s) at the moment you step fully into the swing. While much of throwing good overhands is muscle and determination, being precise is going to get the disc through or over the obstacle you are faced with.

THROWING A HYZER

Being able to control a disc's flight path is essential to accurate throws. A hyzer is a specific type of throw in that you're intentionally forcing the disc to fly in the direction opposite its rotation. For backhanders, throwing a hyzer is fairly easy in that discs tend to naturally fade to this direction anyway, i.e. a right hander's backhand toss will fall left; a left hander's backhand toss will fall right.

Grip

Make a pseudo-fist and press the rim of your driver or approach disc solidly across the inner fold of the palm. Extend your thumb along the top edge of the disc, curl at least three fingers directly underneath, pressing the tips firmly against the disc's inner edge. Now pinch, applying most of the pressure to your thumb and index finger tip. Pinch is everything with a good hyzer (Figure 5.7).

Pinching hard forces your wrist to bend forward so that the

top of your thumb actually begins to pull. It's an awkward position to bend the wrist, so if you're doing it properly you'll definitely feel it. With the disc firmly in your grasp, its farthest edge, it's "nose" if you will, should now be tipped downward. There should be no contact between the disc and your wrist.

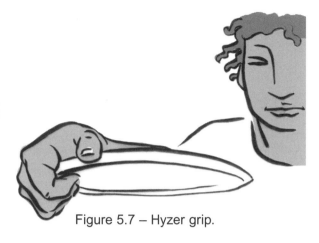

Figure 5.7 – Hyzer grip.

Stance

Again, as with any backhand throw, there's a lot of latitude on initial stance. For a complete discussion on the matter, consult Chapter Seven: Keep Up With Your Approach and Chapter Nine: Finish With Your Drive. In the meantime, just follow the imaginary line that leads from you to the basket.

Windup

It's the backhand again, only this time distinguished by the necessity of keeping the nose of your disc tilted down. Repeat: Keep the nose of the disc tilted down! While failing to keep the nose down will still result in your disc fading left, what you will sacrifice is both control and distance.

Release

Keeping in mind that the intent is to release the disc level, now lift your arm so that the disc is no higher than your shoulders and pointed in the direction of the basket (along the imaginary line). You should now also feel a slight pull along the top of your forearm. If this is the case then you're doing it right. Just remember to strain the top of your thumb to keep the disc pointed down and level when you release, and release it with a snap off your pointer finger.

THROWING AN ANHYZER

The anhyzer (sometimes spelled "anheizer"), like the hyzer, is also a very specific type of throw. With flight characteristics exactly opposite that of the hyzer, throwing an anhyzer forces the disc to actually cut into the direction of its spin, i.e. a right hander's backhand toss will fall right; a left hander's backhand toss will fall left. It's a tough one for most folks to get a handle on because it defies the natural tendency of a backhander's thrown disc to fade the side opposite the throwing arm.

The more stable a disc is, the more self-correcting it is in flight.

Speed of rotation (derived by that ever-important snap!) means everything with the anhyzer toss, as does having an understable disc (see "Understanding Disc Stability" in Chapter Four).

Grip

Make a pseudo-fist and press the rim of your driver or approach disc solidly across the inner fold of the palm. Extend your thumb along the top edge of the disc, curl at least three fingers (probably all four) directly underneath, pressing the tips firmly against the disc's inner edge. Now tilt you wrist up sidewise and back toward the top of your thumb, with the least amount of pressure being applied to the thumb itself (Figure 5.8). The nose of the disc (the edge pointed farthest away) should now be tilted in the direction of your throwing arm, with no contact between the disc and your wrist.

Figure 5.8 – Anhyzer grip.

This is the anhyzer grip.

Stance

Just like with every other backhand throw, there's a lot of lati-tude on initial stance. And yes, for a complete discussion on the matter, consult Chapter Seven and Chapter Nine. Right now, remember the imaginary line linking you to the basket.

Windup

This is the backhand all over again, only this time distin-guished by the necessity of keeping the nose of your disc tilted down and in the direction of your throwing arm. Repeat: Keep the nose of the disc tilted down, slanted in the direction of your throwing arm!

Release

Since the intent of throwing an anyhyzer is to force the disc to cut to the side of your throwing arm – a very challenging feat to pull off – think about the arc of your swing more than anything else. Lift your arm so that the disc is no higher than your shoul-ders and tilt the top plane of the disc in the direction of the bas-ket (along the imaginary line), making the appropriate adjust-ments for angle of ascent and descent. This is how you want your disc positioned when you release.

The arc of your throwing arm during its swing means every-thing to pulling off a successful anhyzer throw. What you really want to do is arc your arm sufficiently to reach the correct release point at the angle and launch.

Don't get too frustrated with the anhyzer. Once you've nailed how to control it, you'll use it often. Time and again it'll save you in situations where you can't rely on your sidearm.

THROWING ROLLERS

Throwing rollers can be both elating and frustrating. Another backhand toss, the roller is defined by the high arc of your throw that enables a disc to land on its edge and roll in the desired direction, usually farther than you could actually throw it any other way. It's a great throw to know (and control) for wooded areas where you need to shimmy a disc under the foliage canopy and between a lot of trunks. Even on an open field the roller has its uses.

A strong roller tends to be shaped like a loose "S", starting at the bottom and worming it's way up to the top. Keep this in mind when targeting the spot you aim to drop your disc.

Grip

The roller grip is the same as for your hyzer toss, at least for the most part. Make a pseudo-fist and press the rim of your driver or approach disc solidly across the inner fold of the palm. Extend your thumb along the top edge of the disc, curl at least three fingers directly underneath, pressing the tips firmly against the disc's inner edge. Apply most of the pressure to your thumb and index finger tip and push down hard (Figure 5.9).

Figure 5.9 – Roller grip.

Pushing down hard, of course, forces your wrist to bend forward so that the top of your thumb actually begins to pull and points the nose of the disc down. There should be no contact between the disc and your wrist.

Stance

Forget about the imaginary line. If you have a pad, step off the pad a few feet with your back to the basket.

Windup

Step onto the pad in a sweeping motion while pivoting – but not directly facing – the basket, and arch your back. You are now facing approximately 45 degrees away from the basket.

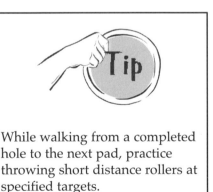

While walking from a completed hole to the next pad, practice throwing short distance rollers at specified targets.

Release

Ahh, release . . . The key to throwing a successful roller is to release the disc at the angle intended to make it roll in the direction you know that the disc will ultimately head for, barring collision with obstacles. Wind, as with every throw, plays a particularly key factor with the roller. Wind can kill it mid-flight, flop it over and land a dud.

Upon release your back should be arched, with your arm steeply inclined in the direction which you wish the disc to touch down and kick off. Keeping in mind the "S" shape that the disc's path will travel, more often than not you'll want to place the disc near the imaginary line extending between the pad and the basket. The disc will kick in the opposite direction of your throwing arm and make you crazy, but finally wend its way back in the direction of the hole. Usually.

For strong throwers, more stable discs are recommended for throwing rollers. For weak throwers, understable discs tend to make for better results. Stable discs are least desirable for throwing rollers, period.

Rollers take time to get down, but have no doubt that once you get it, you'll be on a roll!

FOLLOW-THROUGH

Regardless of what specific shot you're looking to perform, never forget that once the disc releases from your fingertips, you must allow the momentum of your body to expend itself naturally. Don't freeze up just because the disc is in flight, but follow through the motion of your body currently underway and expend the residual energy by allowing your arm to travel past the release point on the imaginary line. By physically following through you will propel the disc more successfully and, more importantly, not strain your arm, blow your shoulder or pull a muscle anywhere else in your body.

Think of it this way: release is the instant you're driving down the freeway and your tire gets punctured and POPS! Follow-through is the moment just afterwards when you brake to the shoulder and listen to all the air hissing out.

SUMMARY

The key to improving your throwing prowess is patience and understanding. By focusing on the individual facets of your technique one at a time (your grip, your stance, your windup, your release) versus trying to master them all at once, what you will discover is a greater sense of how even the most minor adjustments can dramatically impact the outcome. This can be very useful to draw from when attempting to extricate yourself from unexpected situations on the course.

Chapter Six
START WITH YOUR PUTT

You might think it odd, focusing at first on your putting abilities to improve overall game performance. Who cares if you can putt well if it still takes half a dozen throws for you just to reach the pin, right? But here's my thinking. The short game is typically all we've got when we first take up disc golf. Very few people start off as great distance throwers, so let's deal with what you can first manage to do well. And that is throwing your putter into a basket consistently from anywhere within an officially recognized "putting zone" extending ten meters (32 feet 10 inches) from the base of the pin (Figure 6.1).

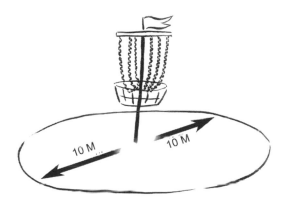

Figure 6.1 – The putting zone.

As your power throws improve, the putts made within this ten meter zone will make or break your game by one or two strokes.

PLAYING SMART

Playing disc golf well requires playing smart. Using the right disc for the right shot is certainly smart, but when it comes to putting, playing smart means knowing when to risk making a hard, long run at a basket from a long distance away, and when to play it safe, laying the disc as near to the putting zone as possible in order to set up the "gimme" putt – the putt that's an automatic sinker. Too often players are compelled to make the "killer" putt, when they're 40 or 50 feet outside the hole, so everybody will give them high-fives. True, if they can just bang some chains and sink that shot it's a beautiful thing, but making such forceful runs at the basket can result not only in missing the chains all together, but also in sending the disc flying so far past the hole that it lands way on the other side of the putting zone. Then what have you got? Yet another hard putt to make, and yet another stroke against you. No high-fivers in that!

Time and again I've seen easy pars blown to double-bogeys (two shots over par for the hole) by showboats trying to make the big birdie play. Know the smart way to take risks. "Drive for show, putt for dough," that's our motto! Putts should never be taken for granted. No matter how close you are to the pin and regardless of how much confidence you have in your skill to plant the disc inside, take the time to remove the disc bag from your shoulder, position yourself properly, and focus clearly on the target. Body balance is a big deal. The weight of a disc bag will throw your balance off and can make you miss even the most no-brainer putts.

Periodic "Killer" putts = OK

Consistent "Gimme" putts = Excellent!

Think smart. Play smart. Take smart risks.

THE PROPER PUTT

Obviously, the proper putt is the one that stays in the basket. Banging some chain, bouncing off the top rim, landing on top of the pin hole but not actually dropping into the basket, none of that means squat to a scorecard, other than adding another stroke against you. Successful putts rely on smoothness, control, and confidence. All three are obtainable with practice and a positive mindset. What can you do to be a sure-shot putter? Let's take a look.

There are three standard approaches to successful putting technique, each amendable to what works best for you. Being comfortable and adept at all of them will serve you well on the course, given the myriad of predicaments you'll see.

A disc that strikes the side of the basket, gets stuck there and doesn't fall to the ground, counts as being inside the basket.

Figure 6.2 – Straddle putt stance.

STRADDLE PUTT

With the straddle putt, stand facing the basket with your feet spread squarely, about shoulder-width apart (or wider). Now picture a straight line leading from your belly button to the pin and relax your knees a bit (Figure 6.2).

FOOT-FORWARD PUTT

With the foot-forward putt, stand facing the basket with one foot behind the other like you're taking a step toward it, with the toes of the forward foot pointed directly at the pin. The imaginary straight line leads from your front foot and is funneled out your belly button directly to the basket (Figure 6.3).

SIDE-STRADDLE PUTT

The side-straddle putt is geared mostly for long distance putts over 40 or 50 feet in distance with emphasis on an anhyzer. Stand facing the basket with one foot behind the other as though you're taking a step toward it,

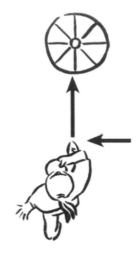

Figure 6.3 – Foot-forward putt stance.

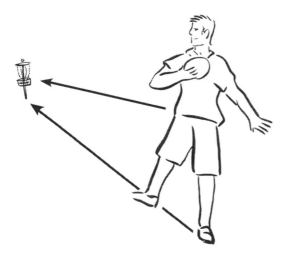

Figure 6.4 – Side straddle putt stance.

then pivot 45 degrees away from the basket. Both your feet and shoulders should be on the imaginary straight line leading from you to the basket (Figure 6.4).

Regardless of which technique is adopted as a personal preference, there are certain things to keep them in mind whenever you're putting.

1. Relax
2. Get your balance
3. Focus
4. Visualize the disc getting into the basket
5. Use your wrist
6. *Visualize the disc getting into the basket!*

MAKING THE PUTT

Whether playing recreationally or in a tournament, there's a tendency to place a lot of pressure on making the putt. In tourney play the pressure can be even greater because there's a 30 second time limit in which to throw, after the previous player has thrown and the distractions have been eliminated. This is where playing smart comes in. First, be confident that the putt you're trying to sink is a makable shot. That said, the first thing you want to do is select the right disc for the job.

SELECTING THE RIGHT PUTTER

As with drivers and approach discs, there are a variety of putters to choose from. Knowing which disc to use to do the right job is a fundamental part of improving your overall gameplay performance.

There are over 20 types of putting discs available on the market, nearly all uniquely distinguished by their shape and composition. Stability factors into putter design, certainly, but most conspicuous are the variety of lip and dome characteristics.

Many putters look and feel much like your typical approach discs, featuring a modest dome, a more rounded edge, and a weighty lip. What they're really all about is stability. Some are much more square-lipped, with higher domes which tend to make them float in the air, and still others have virtually no dome at all and are squared off on the edge.

Wind conditions, which we'll get into in a moment, factor heavily in making accurate putts, so keep this in mind when reaching for your putter.

My primary putter is heavy and stable, so that it's very dependable in breezy conditions. For longer distance putts in non-windy conditions, and for making trick shots around trees or from under tight spots, I often reach for a floater, which I can throw farther with less effort. Given the situation, even the odd approach disc will sometimes work.

BALANCE

Once you've determined the position from which you'll shoot, and you've thought of the putting techniques best suited for the situation, plant your feet as solidly on the ground as possible to acquire maximum balance. While you're not allowed to remove obstacles that may impair your ability to reach or extend your arm for a throw, you can kick away rocks and sticks and leaves that might effect your stance stability. Just try not to kick them at somebody! What you can and can't do during gameplay is listed in the official *PDGA Rules of Play*.

Having good balance is key to putting accurately. Although you don't move your feet as you do with so many a windup, generally there is significant shifting of body weight in order to propel the disc forcefully. Remember that solid putting mostly comes down to smooth arm and wrist motion. Your center of gravity has a lot to do with getting your putter successfully across the distance between you and the basket. If you think of your belly button as the spot from which all action springs, it's easy to understand.

As your center of gravity points directly at the hole (at least with the straddle and foot-forward techniques), your body weight will naturally shift toward it as you rock forward to the point of disc release. What this enables you to do is exert less effort to get the disc across the distance needed to hit the hole.

I do mean "rock" and not step forward. It is against regulation to step past the putting position until the disc has gone where it's going. Stepping forward indicates that you lost control of the putt, and stepping over the lie is called a "falling putt" for which you will be penalized.

FOCUS

Focus is everything with a sure putt. I don't mean just clearing your mind of the distractions around you – the silent, willful stares of the other players (and not necessarily in your favor), the smack of trees being walloped elsewhere on the course, the distant cries of "Fore!" (or worse). I mean finding a place on the pin on which to fix your eyes, and not taking your eyes off that spot. That is your target. A specific chain link is a good target, as is just off-center of the rod strip of tape marking the middle of the pin amid the chains. Focusing off center is extremely important.

When tossing a putt the disc will hit the chains and kick in the opposite direction of its rotation. What this means for a right hander is that a disc that hits the chains on the left side of the pin will often kick out to the left and miss the basket below. Likewise, a left hander's disc that strikes chain on the right side of the pin will

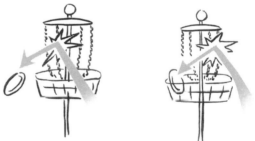

Figure 6.5 – Putt into opposite side of pole to avoid kicking out.

kick right and out. The thing to do is focus on the same side of the pin as your throwing arm so that the disc's kick will be into the chains, which will serve to stop its flight path, ensnare the disc, and drop it into basket (Figure 6.5). It never hurts to put a little anhyzer on your disc as well, so that it curves in the direction of your throwing arm.

WATCH THE WIND

Seriously consider wind direction every time you set up to putt. Even the slightest breeze can adversely affect the flight path of a disc. For instance, when throwing into the wind the disc will lift above its intended trajectory and travel much higher and farther than you intend; when releasing with the wind behind you, the disc will be pushed downward from your release point and inevitably fall short of the intended trajectory. Couple this with the fact that every type of disc handles wind situations differently (most notably the Blow Fly which has a concave belly making it especially susceptible to breeze influence, resulting in erratic, highly unpredictable behavior) and you've got a challenge.

To judge wind direction, snatch up a handful of grassy bits and drop them into the air. If it's especially breezy and you are putting into the wind, putt hard and straight at the middle of the chains (Figure 6.6a). Otherwise the disc will lift over the top of the basket. Many pro-standard courses have pin holes with flags attached to the top that can also help you judge wind direction.

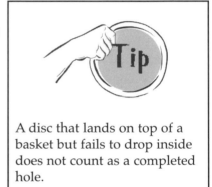

A disc that lands on top of a basket but fails to drop inside does not count as a completed hole.

If you are putting with the wind behind you, compensate by putting high, at or over the top of the basket, depending on wind velocity. The disc will drop abruptly at some point between you and the hole (Figure 6.6b).

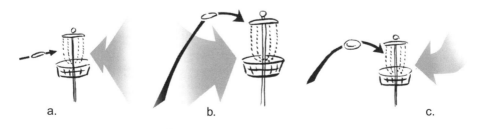

a.   b.   c.

Figure 6.6 – Wind effects on putts.

If the wind is coming at you from the side, slightly tilt the top-side of the disc into the wind and compensate by playing the arc of the disc's flight path or tossing straight and hard to cut through the wind (Figure 6.6c). Slanting the underside of the disc toward the wind will result in its being carried away.

GET A RIGHT GRIP

The grip to use when making a putt is vastly different from both the drive and approach grips. While your putting grip needs to be firm, it should be slightly looser than any power grip you might be using with other throws. Also, finger placement beneath the disc is relatively wider, middle finger extended, in order to keep the plane of the disc fixed on its intended flight path, with the thumb generally set back from the edge so that there are three pressure points (Figure 6.7).

Figure 6.7 – Adjusted putting grip.

Do not place your pointer finger length-wise along the disc's lip, which is a very common mistake. When the putter rotates out of the hand at its release point, the pointer finger will spring back at the last moment against the momentum of the disc and knock it slightly off kilter, throwing it off its intended trajectory. Focus totally on your target spot and putt firmly with confidence.

Imagine the straight line between you and the basket, focus on that specific spot you envision your putter disc hitting, and don't take your eyes off your target before release of the disc. A lot of people glance down at the top ring of the basket at the last instant and that's inevitably where their disc hits. Focus and smooth, quality wrist action is vital when striving to improve your putting technique. Upon release, try to work in a little disc wobble to help prevent the disc from crashing through the chains and traveling completely past the basket.

There's so little wind-up with a putt that you might assume follow-through would not be necessary. But that final burst of energy which propels the disc from your hand – your spring release – needs to be expelled, so do allow your arm to extend fluidly beyond release into full extension.

SUMMARY

Putting accurately and consistently is the key to shaving strokes off your game. The quickest way to improving your putting skills is to practice as often as you can. While many courses have a basket set aside for player warm up at the beginning of a round, you can also simply set up a target at home, maybe a chair or laundry basket, and devote time to routinely hitting the target from within ten meters. Your ultimate aim should be to make such putts a no-brainer activity, something so comfortable and automatic that you'll never freeze up from the pressure to hit the basket on the course.

I recommend that you practice putting with your putters and approach discs only and forget about using your drivers. You will not be putting with your drivers so why bother banging them up needlessly and having to change your throw every time you practice?

And don't obsess with trying to improve your 40 and 50 foot killer putts. You won't, at least not enough to make a measurable difference in your game in the short term. It's the smart player who plants the disc within the putting zone and knows that what is required is practiced, skillful disc control, not luck, to plant the putter in the basket.

Chapter Seven
KEEP UP WITH YOUR APPROACH

By improving your short game in the beginning, you can compensate greatly for whatever distance you're unable to achieve when first driving off the pad. Making consistently accurate mid-range shots will help accomplish this. The ultimate goal, of course, is to throw the approach disc within the ten meter putting zone to set up that sure-shot putt you know you can make. Wrap your mind around making par for the hole and play it one hole at a time.

Become comfortable with technique and become familiar with the differing flight characteristics of the discs at your disposal.

Let everybody else sweat out the long-drive birdie runs. Your goal should simply be to keep your shots on the fairway while progressing steadily toward the hole. Do this and, coupled with your increased putting finesse, you'll be surprised just how easy it is to hold your own with those players who haven't devoted time and attention to playing smart.

Let's dissect the approach shot.

A "worm burner" is a shot released downward that lands prematurely.

WHAT YOU CAN DO

The first thing to know about throwing an approach shot is that in order to throw, you don't have to stand rigid above the spot where your previous disc landed. One thing is true – you must ultimately have one supporting point of the body within 30 centimeters of the exact spot where your disc last landed. You are allowed to start from farther behind so you can step up to that spot to throw. In fact, you could probably run up and do a cartwheel beforehand,

Figure 7.1 – Step up to the lie to bolster momentum and distance.

just so long as you end up on the lie before you release the disc! The biggest benefit of stepping up to the lie is so that you can windup sufficiently to get some rip on your disc before release (Figure 7.1).

MARKING THE LIE

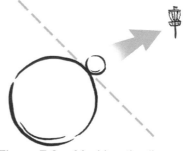

The easiest way to determine where your foot is supposed to go when throwing your approach is to simply pick up the landed disc and plant your foot there. Usually nobody has a problem with doing this during recreational play. In tourney competi-

Figure 7.2 – Marking the lie.

tion, however, failing to mark your lie properly will not only cost you a penalty stroke, but also rob you of extra room to put your foot closer to the hole. And hey, that extra few inches can make a world of difference.

The proper (and expected) way to mark the lie is to use a mini-marker disc. Before picking up your thrown disc from where it landed, place the mini-marker directly on the playing field between it and the hole, making sure their edges are touching (Figure 7.2). Once finished, you may retrieve your thrown disc to either use again or bag.

The area measuring 30 centimeters behind the mini-marker is where you must ultimately have one supporting point of your body, i.e. your foot or knee, upon release of the disc. Do not pick up the mini-marker until after you've thrown. If it's accidentally moved before you throw, you must put it back in its original position.

In a situation like getting a disc stuck in a tree, the mini-marker is placed directly beneath where the disc got stuck (Figure 7.3).

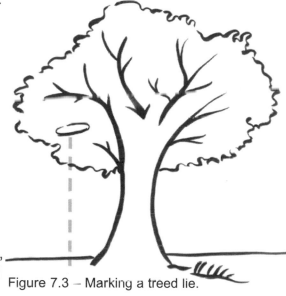

Figure 7.3 – Marking a treed lie.

GETTING WHERE YOU WANT TO BE

The number one goal of the approach toss (or up-shot) is getting your disc in close enough proximity to the basket to make the putt. Unlike drives off the pad, where accuracy can be compromised to some degree in order to achieve maximum distance in pursuit of a birdie, the approach shot is all about playing the angles well. Controlling accuracy comes only from having smoothness in your windup, release and follow-through. And the only way to achieve smoothness is through repetition, and repetition is defined by lots and lots of practice. We'll get into how you can best practice in a minute, but now let's look at playing the angles.

PLAYING THE ANGLES

Playing the angles simply means knowing the arc of your disc's flight path. Flight path is most often determined by your choice of disc to throw and how you throw it. But knowing in advance how the disc will respond in flight will allow you to exploit its fade (the direction of its arc as its rotation slows) and plant it where you want it to go. So rarely is disc golf a game of merely throwing discs straight and level (what with all the mandatories, the dog-legs, the water hazards and other obstacles that can impair your path), a successful approach mostly comes down to having keen focus and total control of your hyzer and anhyzer techniques.

Most of your throws will naturally fade in the opposite direction of your throwing arm (hyzer), so use this knowledge to your benefit on approach. Remember that with your approach shots distance is secondary and accuracy is number one. Many make the mistake of focusing only on the basket itself on approach and end up chucking a disc far to the wrong side of the goal. My advice: do not throw at the basket so much as to the side of it, as far out as needed, on the side of your throwing arm. Why? Because the natural arc of the disc's flight path will bring it down on the far side of the imaginary straight line extending from your hand at the point of release.

Picture a bicycle wheel with all its spokes, then cut it in half across the middle and trash the bottom. With only the top half of the wheel, now picture yourself as the axle from which the remaining spokes lead. Picture the top of the spoke leading straight up as where the pin basket lies. By understanding which direction your throw is going to fade and what adjustments to make to the disc's angle of release, you can now view the other

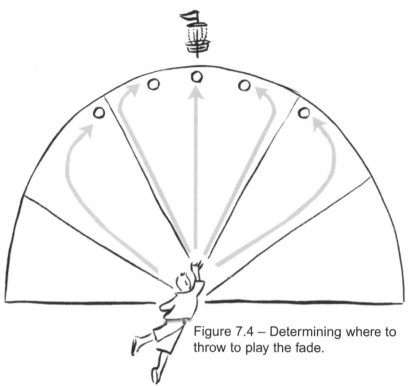

Figure 7.4 – Determining where to throw to play the fade.

spokes as your line of sight (the imaginary straight line extending from your hand at the point on which to release) (Figure 7.4).

Here's how it works: Extend your throwing arm fully in the direction of the "spoke" you've chosen to be the intended flight path. Clearly visualize where you want your disc to be as it travels along the chosen "spoke," where you want it to begin its fade and where you want it to hit the ground. With your natural hyzer throw, it's likely the disc will skip when touching down, so keep this in mind. In fact, see the entire play clearly in your mind before you throw. It's very easy during those precious few milliseconds separating windup and release to focus on the basket itself and inadvertently

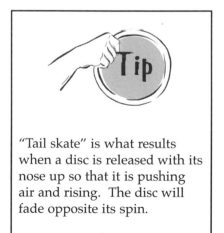

Tip

"Tail skate" is what results when a disc is released with its nose up so that it is pushing air and rising. The disc will fade opposite its spin.

throw straight at it. What happens then is your disc may end up way off course, and you'll lose at least one stroke just to get back on. Do take into account whether the fairway is sloped or not. A hyzer-thrown disc will often hit the ground on a slope and roll uncontrollably.

THINGS TO CONSIDER

While playing the fade is all about knowing what angles to use when releasing the disc to get you where you want to be, what disc you opt to use is a huge contributor to the outcome. Drivers, particularly ultra-long-range drivers, are not the discs you generally want to be using on approach. They tend to be more slim than your approach discs and often feature a more streamlined edge so they'll skip much farther when touching down. Approach discs usually stick fairly close to where they hit. There are situations where using flatter, harder discs can really come in handy because of their predictable skip, but generally use your most comfortable mid-range disc to consistently get the job done.

WIND FACTOR

Among the many mitigating factors that can affect any shot, let alone your approach, is wind. Wind, wind, wind, invariably, will either help or hinder your best efforts to make a quality toss. Wind just blows me away, frankly, but on some occasions the wind is actually an ally.

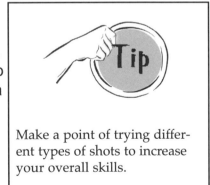

Make a point of trying different types of shots to increase your overall skills.

You've got to learn to play in wind. So these are the things to remember when approaching in windy or even just breezy conditions:

1. Wind always affects the arc of your disc's flight path so you must compensate accordingly.
2. Wind direction can vary drastically and unpredictably between you and the hole, so throw low whenever possible.

3. Wind blows!

While the angle of release determines the arc of the flight path which follows, it is grip and rip that make the flight path actually happen, particularly in windy conditions. When wind is blowing from the side of your throwing arm and you have to cut into it with an anhyzer, the disc will be pushed down and back, so for a right hander, you may want to throw higher and more right if you can't make a direct run at the target. Throwing into wind blowing from the opposite side of your throwing arm (a hyzer shot) will cause your disc to push back and lift up. If you don't have enough downward angle on the nose, the disc might very well turn over and be carried off completely. (Figure 7.5)

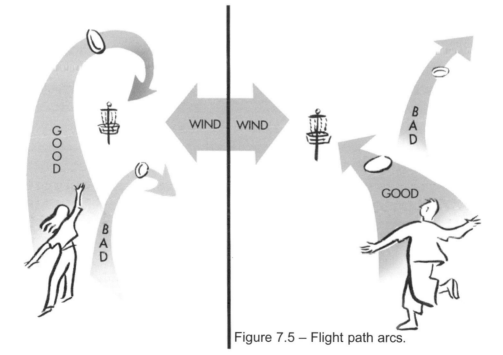

Figure 7.5 – Flight path arcs.

Even in mildly breezy conditions try to keep the disc as level to the ground as possible to avoid losing control. A final thing about throwing in wind: use heavier discs – stable, overstable only. Light discs thrown in windy conditions (your 150- and 160-

gram classes) are out of control the moment they leave your hand, unless you know how to throw them.

SUMMARY

Good approaches keep you in the game. If you really want to get better with your approaches, then practice somewhere other than on a disc golf course. The course is for gameplay and a good time so that's where your head should be when you're out there, intent on getting your best score by taking it just one hole at a time. But practice warrants quality time and mental focus. Find yourself a clearing where you can safely toss some discs without beaning somebody, start short and gradually progress to longer distance tosses. Get at least three to five similar approach discs, maybe of varying weights. Pick a spot you want to hit and go for it. Start with your hyzer shots. Next go for your anhyzer shots, and finally work on your straight line drive shots, slinging low and level. Every successful pro player has a solidly consistent line-drive, so why shouldn't you?

As your technique improves and you acquire greater control and understanding of the discs' performance, start throwing farther by selecting more distant targets. As your controlled distance shots improve you'll find yourself ready to tackle the biggest buggaboo of 'em all — improving your drive!

Chapter Eight
FINISH WITH YOUR DRIVE

Having nailed your putts and fine tuned your approaches, now you're ready to tackle what is possibly the single most vexing of all aspects of disc golf: making the most of your driving potential. Like Hydra, the multi-headed serpent of myth, the long distance drive can also be an elusive many-headed beast to wrangle. Slaying this beast in your effort to discover the technique that is right for you will be no small challenge.

What exactly is the best way to squeeze maximum distance out of your drivers? The discs themselves are a big part of the equation, as is grip, run-up, windup, extension, release, snap, follow-through and anything else you want to talk about. It seems just about everybody who's been disc'n it awhile has a very distinct and passionate view on what (and what not) to do on the pad. Do not despair in this exasperating quest for improvement. Determining which technique or combination of techniques will ultimately work best for you is going to require experimentation and practice.

WHERE TO START

Here's what you want to achieve: birdies and aces. But not every hole you play warrants the big power, long-distance drive. Short holes require good skill, yet far less oomph to reach. You need to consider not only the distance needed to reach the basket, but also the obstacles that lay between you and the basket, and the most feasible path to get you there successfully.

In the beginning, placing a drive anywhere even near the basket area of your longer holes can seem a pretty daunting task. When you watch the big throwers routinely plant their drives well into the putting zone, it can even be disheartening. They often make it look so effortless, while you're cranking everything you've got into just getting your disc half as far! The thing to remember about these players and their drives is that they've gotten their technique down and they know which discs to use for each situation. Watch them closely, ask questions, and learn from them as you go along. Take whatever advice you can get and put it into practice to figure out if it's useful to you. What you should do in the meanwhile is endeavor to drive smart – just like with your approaches and putts.

Your primary objectives when driving are being cool, staying in control of the disc, and keeping it on the fairway. Size up the hole and determine what alternate routes there may be for you to make the shot successfully. Lots of holes you encounter will be fairly straightforward – flat open-field courses where it's simply a matter of throwing long, straight and level (a challenge in itself!). Then there are those with plenty of obstacles that often

provide a host of options – and opportunities. Should you maybe throw a hyzer high and wide over the trees? Skip low and through? Roll it? How about sidearm an anhyzer from the opposite side? The wisest thing you can do is to pick the play that exploits your strengths. Possessing a variety of controlled, confident drives really comes in handy.

Remember to stretch your back, arms and legs before driving off your first hole.

Remember, use the right disc for the right job at the right time!

WHAT TO CONSIDER WHEN SELECTING DRIVERS

The right driver to use varies from player to player. While some can power throw twice the distance that you can, there are a couple of ways to compensate while initially developing your skills. Using hard-plastic or specially coated discs can help. Given the reliability of their tremendous skipping capacity, by playing the skip you can often add at least another 10 to 30 feet of distance to your drive. Another thing you can do is buy lighter weight discs.

Weight-wise, a lot of players today are using the 170 class weights, which is what I started playing with. I'm not a big guy, but I reckoned I was strong enough to use this class, so I routinely bought anywhere from 171 to 176-gram discs. Despite my improvement in technique, I remained unsatisfied with the inconsistent gain I was getting on my drives, and I questioned whether the weight class was just too heavy for me.

I bought both a 155-gram and 166-gram disc and experimented. Everything changed for me that very day. I was throwing farther, consistently controlling flight paths, and feeling like someone who actually knew what he was doing on the pad! Though it can certainly be argued that better technique would've made up for whatever strength I lacked when first developing my driving skills – and I still do use my 170s a lot – the 160 class is what I now drive with most often. In addition to the lighter weights improving my gameplay, they allowed me to focus more clearly on all the differing aspects of technique that I couldn't concentrate on with the feeling of heaviness in my hand.

Give it a try and see what you think.

BREAKING IT DOWN

Don't try to fix everything at once. It's better to work on your techniques just one step at a time, in the order most suited to your needs. Break it down to the following:
- grip
- windup

- arm extension
- release point
- snap
- follow-through

The ability to combine all these things into a seamless throw will take some practice. Devote sufficient time to each step of the process individually, get comfortable enough with it so that it becomes a matter of rote, then progress to the next step. You'll have not only a clearer understanding of what works and what doesn't, but most importantly you'll also have an understanding of why something works for you. By firmly establishing the unique physical aspects of every step and connecting them systematically, you'll develop a comfortable, flowing rhythm that will give you the automated control needed for you to then concentrate on maximizing distance.

ADDING DISTANCE TO YOUR DRIVE

The big long-distance rip is the throw nearly everybody wants to master. For some folks it comes easily, for most of us it does not. You'll hear many theories on the secret to making the great long-distance drive. Many will claim it's all about the snap, putting more spin on the disc in order to hold its line longer. Others will say it's all in the windup. Still others believe it's in the run-up that's so much a part of the windup for many. What it really comes down to is the correct combination of efficient execution of any and all of these things, plus body control, quick twitch, and strong central body muscles. Timing definitely figures into it; and you can't forget that what works for some might not necessarily work best for you. Still, there are certain components invariably inherent to making the successful long-distance drive.

In Chapter Four we discussed the distinction between throwing a golf disc properly and throwing a Frisbee. With driving I'd mentioned to keep your arm fairly straight, using little wrist action. The intent of this approach is to break the habit of tossing like one typically does a Frisbee. The result is that many players develop a semi-circular driving action that resembles a sort of wheel, at least once you factor in the pivot of the body as it steps into release position. While this method works fine and provides sufficient momentum and control of the disc, the one downside is that it fails to produce a fixed position for releasing the disc. Given the variation of release points – even just a fraction of an inch either way – throwing the disc precisely in the direction you intend can prove challenging.

For both accuracy and distance most of your major league drivers use a motion similar to that of trying to start a lawn mower (gas powered, not electric), which is by yanking the rip cord handle attached to the starter. The fact that it's called a "rip" cord is most appropriate, too.

Or just think of snapping a wet towel. It's the same motion.

Target your path and determine your release point. Picture the straight line leading from you to the basket (or whatever path you've chosen) and step to your starting position, pulling your back pretty much to the basket. You should start relatively straight, along the same line as that of the "wheel" method of throwing, but this time as you take the steps and pivot the body into its release position, pull your arm straight across your chest – like yanking the rip cord of the lawn mower – keeping your elbow close and the disc consistent with the imaginary line you're traveling on. Having already established the path's target at the beginning, the release point is now fixed; it is exactly 180

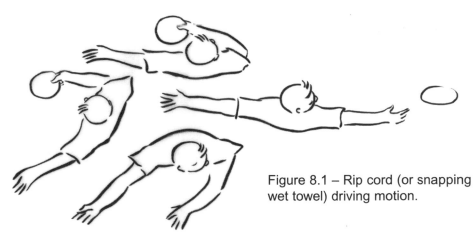

Figure 8.1 – Rip cord (or snapping wet towel) driving motion.

degrees from where you began your windup (Figure 8.1).

Wrist movement during the final micro-moments preceding release is what produces the snap so important to ripping a disc hard. What makes a disc fly farther has a lot to do with the speed of its rotation during flight. That final snap of the wrist is what produces that speed, so don't curl up too early. A good snap should make your pointer finger sting!

THE RUN-UP THAT WORKS

The number of footsteps you should incorporate into your windup run-up is nothing to be taken lightly, and the correct answer may only be determined by you. Some players require very little footwork while many others prefer using the 180 degree pivot, and still others – particularly many title-holding pros – start facing the direction they intend to throw and then do a complete 360 before disc release.

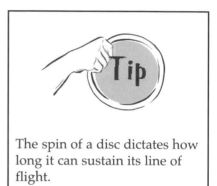

The spin of a disc dictates how long it can sustain its line of flight.

I'm not much of an advocate for the half-step windup for a drive, primarily because I'm just no good at it. To me, every little bit of extra momentum the body contributes by propelling itself forward provides not only extra zing to the release, but also allows just a smidgen more time to get the adrenaline pumping, psyche up sufficiently, and totally focus on control of the disc's release. Also, I think there's something to be said about the motion of moving forward in general: you're moving forward, so naturally the disc wants to go forward. In fact, I like to think that I'm merely inhibiting the disc's innate desire to go much farther than I can throw it to begin with!

THE 180 RUN-UP

The 180 run-up typically consists of three steps. Having determined the intended angle and point of disc release, the player stands facing away from the target along the imaginary line leading toward it (Figure 8.2).

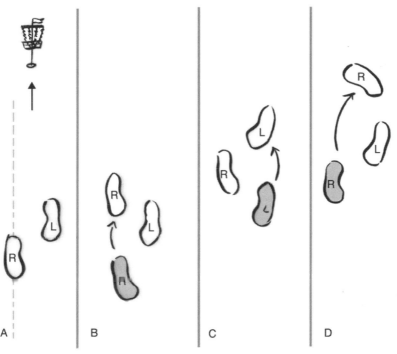

Figure 8.2 – 180 degree foot positions.

(A) Stand with your back to the basket. The foot of the throwing arm side should be positioned forward on the line, the other placed at least a half-step behind.

(B) Initiate the run-up by stepping back with your leading foot.

(C) On the second step continue along the imaginary line and tense up on your grip of the disc.

(D) Swivel your hips into the third step while still facing away from the basket and raise your elbow to pull the disc inward toward your chest. As the throwing side foot lands on the imaginary line, in one swift motion yank the disc close past your chest and extend your arm fully to the release point with a snap of the wrist.

THE 360 RUN-UP

The 360 run-up also consists of three steps for a lot of players, and many many more steps for others. For simplicity we'll stick with the three-step method. Having determined the intended angle and point of disc release, the player stands facing the target along the imaginary line leading toward it. The foot opposite the throwing arm side should be positioned forward, the other placed at least a half step behind (Figure 8.3).

(1) Initiate the run-up by stepping forward with your throwing side foot on a near-45 degree pivot.

(2) On the second step continue the sweep of the pivot another 45 degrees so that you now face away from the basket and tense up your disc grip.

(3) Pivot back around on the third step in a complete 180, raising your elbow and pulling the disc inward toward the chest. As your throwing side foot lands on the imaginary line, in one swift motion yank the disc close past your chest and extend your arm fully to the release point with a snap of the wrist.

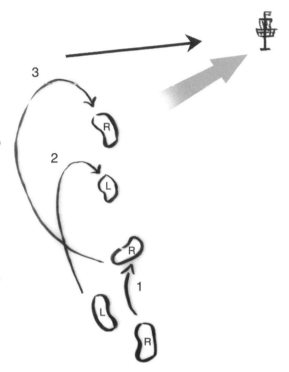

Figure 8.3 – 360 degree foot positions.

Choose whichever method of run-up that works best for you. Good balance and timing are essential, but keep in mind that while the physics of forward motion necessarily result in additional forward energy being transferred to the disc to help it go a little farther, the amount of energy it adds is probably negligible. The real force behind a disc comes from the speed of your arm pull through extension and release, and the snap of your wrist to increase spin.

For some players such run-ups only confuse the issue of control and accuracy of release – just too many things to coordinate quickly. If that's the case with you, then don't do a big, con-voluted run-up. Watch what others do, experiment and improvise until it all comes together. What is most important is that you focus on your pull and release.

PULL AND RELEASE

The bulk of the power propelling a disc is generated by the speed of your arm pull through release – your rip – with the snap of wrist providing the spin that'll determine its length and stability of flight. Do not confuse arm speed with power of muscle strength.

Think of the motion used to snap a wet towel when moving through your driving action.

There is a tendency to be standing on the pad, faced with a long hole, and to just chuck a disc as hard as you can in order to get it where it needs to go. Even with outstanding technique, more often than not this brute strength approach to driving will result in the sacrifice of total control of your disc. Great technique is not so essential with the major hammer throws, where arm and shoulder strength determine how high and how far you can chuck a disc before its momentum drops out from under it. But for controlled backhand shots, good technique is a must. You will often find that by not strong-arming a drive with all your might, by pulling back just a little so you can focus on your technique, you will retain greater control of the disc and generally throw farther and with greater accuracy.

SUMMARY

Learning how to drive exceptionally well may be a long process. There are many different things to keep in mind when determining the correct backhand technique that will work best for you. As with approach shots and putts, consistent practice and regular play can easily make all the difference in improving game scores.

Talk to other players, experiment and adapt, bulld your throwing repertoire, and enjoy. One day you'll step onto the course and completely surprise yourself with how your game is going. Really, it will happen!

Chapter Nine
RULES & ETIQUETTE

It's no wonder why disc golf's popularity continues to grow. Disc'n is cool, it's easy-going, it's challenging, you are outside and having fun and so utterly filled with good vibes that there's very little reason to get bent out of shape. I mean really just how seriously can you take slinging discs all day long in the sun with a bunch of friends? Well, truth be told, pretty seriously.

People of all ages from every walk of life seem to be playing disc golf these days. One of the reasons is because generally respectful manners are demonstrated by most everyone. It's important that you use common sense and do likewise when you're playing too. Just like Sir Paul McCartney said (no doubt talking about disc golf), "The love you take is equal to the love you make!"

GENERAL RULES & CONDUCT

For a comprehensive listing of the rules governing gameplay, you can get a copy of the Professional Disc Golf Association's booklet, *Complete Rules of Play*. While all rules are strictly enforced during tournament competition and should generally be practiced by players at all times, during recreational gameplay most folks observe only the basics (that is until they buy a copy of the booklet and stick it in their bag). That said, here are the most common courtesies and regulations to observe when you're on the course:

WHEN DRIVING

• Who throws first on Hole One?

Flip a coin if you want to, because in recreational play it really doesn't matter who throws first. In tournament play where there are several groups of players, generally a throwing order list is determined in advance and the different groups are assigned specific holes to start from. For instance, hole four might be where your group begins its round, and the course is completed by playing through to hole three.

• Who throws first next?

The player who threw the least number of times during the last hole goes first on the next hole. If everyone threw an equal number of times, assume the same rotation as the preceding tee.

• How much time do I have to throw?

A player is allowed no more than 30 seconds to throw a disc once marking the lie, presuming the playing field is clear of distractions.

• Where do I stand when somebody else is driving?

When possible, stand behind or to the rear side of the tee pad to provide as little distraction to the driver as possible.

• Are "mulligans" allowed?

Mulligans (extra throws) are not allowed in professional play. In recreational play, however, it is entirely up to you. Many people like to have the option of having one available mulligan per round. It is best to discuss mulligan policy with your group before gameplay begins.

• Can I step off the tee to throw?

Upon disc release, both feet must be in contact with the teeing surface. After disc release, stepping off the pad during follow-through is allowed.

- **Can I start my run-up off the tee?**
  Yes, it is permissible to begin your run-up from off and behind the teeing area.

- **What if the group ahead is treed or has lost a disc?**
  If somebody's disc is stuck in a tree in front of you and they are not waving you through, warn them that you are driving through and proceed only when it's safe to do so.

- **What is a "mandatory"?**
  Any area that officially designates the flight path a disc must travel in order to reach the hole is called a mandatory. Should a disc travel past the mandatory area but not go directly through it, the player must throw back to the front of the designated area, then throw through it properly.

WHEN APPROACHING

- **Who throws first?**
  The away player, the one whose lie is farthest away from the hole, plays first.

- **Where do I stand?**
  Try to remain behind another player's field of vision when possible, so as not to distract his or her concentration. If that's not possible, stand still.

- **How do I mark the lie?**
  The official way to mark the lie is to place a mini marker disc on the playing surface in front of the thrown disc, touching its edge, directly in line between it and the hole. During recreational play, many people just put their foot on the spot where the thrown disc landed, or flip the laid disc over on it's forward-most edge to mark the play line.

- **What if my disc is stuck in a tree?**
  A disc stuck in a tree (or any other obstacle) at a height of

over two meters (six feet, six inches) above the playing surface counts as one penalty stroke against you. The lie is marked directly below where the disc became stuck.

• **How do I get my disc out of a tree?**

Do not use other discs in effort to retrieve a disc stuck in a tree or you will only get more discs stuck in a tree. If you're unable to climb the tree or shake the disc loose, and only if it's safe to do so, throw objects at it in an effort to knock it loose. I recommend carrying a golf ball or hockey puck in your bag specifically for this purpose.

• **What if my disc rests on the out-of-bounds line?**

In the event a disc comes to rest on or against the out-of-bounds line, it is permissible to mark the lie one meter (three feet, three inches) away from and perpendicular to the line, even if it takes the lie closer to the pin. Determine which side of the out-of-bounds line a disc is on by where the largest portion of the disc rests.

• **What if I go out-of-bounds?**

When a disc goes out-of-bounds, regardless of where it lands, the lie is declared at the relative spot where the disc first went out-of-bounds. The player receives a one-stroke penalty for each out-of-bounds occurrence.

• **What if there is something impairing my ability to throw?**

You may not move any permanent obstacle that interferes with your ability to throw. If you find yourself standing in a bush, or have a tree branch in front of you, you are not allowed to bend it out of the way. It is okay if you make incidental contact with the obstruction during your throw.

• **What if I land in water?**

If you land in water, the lie will be on the shoreline directly across from where the disc splashed down, at least as near as can be determined. Getting your disc out while staying dry is the real problem!

- **What if I lose my disc?**

In the event you can't find your disc, determine the approximate location where it became lost and mark the lie. In addition to a lost disc, it'll cost you a one-stroke penalty. In tourney play, by the way, you have only three minutes to recover a disc.

- **How long do I have to throw?**

A player is allowed no more than 30 seconds to throw a disc once marking the lie, presuming the playing field is clear of distractions.

WHEN PUTTING

- **What is the putting zone?**

The putting zone is the area surrounding the basket, extending 10 meters (32 feet, 10 inches) from the pole.

- **Who throws first?**

As with all shots following the drive, the away player (the one whose disc is farthest from the hole) throws first.

- **What is a "falling putt"?**

Unlike with approach shots, where a player can cross the lie as part of his or her natural follow-through (post disc release) a putting player must demonstrate total control of balance upon release of the disc and remain in front of the lie. While putting, if any supporting point of the player's body crosses the lie, the putt is considered a falling putt and may result in a penalty.

- **Do I have to remove my disc from the basket before another player putts?**

During recreational play it is not deemed necessary to remove your disc from the basket before others have putted. In tournament competition, it is expected.

- **What if the disc lands on top of the basket?**

A disc that comes to rest on top of the basket is not considered to actually be in the basket, thus does not count as a successful putt.

- **What if the disc sticks in the side of the basket?**

A disc that lodges itself in the side of the basket below the top ring and fails to fall to the ground is considered a valid, successful putt.

COMMON COURTESY

Using common sense and good judgement, showing appropriate respect, and simply being considerate at all times bolsters everybody's enjoyment of gameplay. Here are some of the things to remember and put into practice:

DONT'S

- Don't scream foul language when a toss goes awry. Disc golf for many is a family pastime and there are often children present. Not everybody needs or appreciates hearing cuss words screamed at the top of your lungs just because you may possess a refined ability to use them!

- Don't litter. Disc golf courses are often on public park land and probably not huge money-makers for their municipalities. Factor in the litigious society in which we live and that heavy plastic discs flying everywhere can pose a hazard to civilians, and I'm sure you'll agree we must always endeavor to present the sport in its best possible light. Thwart those that would have our land used for lawn bowling!

- Don't let your dog roam free. If the course you're playing on allows you to bring a dog – which is way cool – then keep it on a leash so it doesn't go romping over to other players and interfere with their game (or take off with their discs). And definitely clean up after your dog because, well, discs get slippery!

- Don't get grumpy. Maintain a positive attitude because bad vibes are contagious and often directly affect the enjoyment of those playing around you.

- Don't be a "Chatty Cathy." When playmates or others nearby are trying to concentrate on a pending throw, then be quiet and try not to distract them.

- When introducing others to the sport, don't try to fix everything they're doing wrong on every hole. Make a periodic suggestion that may improve their performance if they want it, but in the beginning it should really be about friends discovering for themselves all the joy to be found in disc golf. There's plenty of time for them to improve their game later.

DOS
- Do be aware of those playing behind you. If you get treed or lose a disc and there's a group at the pad, then allow them to play through.

- Do be conscientious of those playing in front of you. Throwing before they've cleared the hole may result in an injury or bad vibes.

- Do yell "clear" when you've finished a hole and the group behind you can't see the basket.

- Do stay alert for incoming discs. It hurts to get beaned by one!

- Do yell "fore" any time there's a possibility of your disc hitting somebody.

- Do alert those in front of you who have become treed or lost a disc that you're driving through before you do so.
- Do ask large, slow groups if you can play through if you are by yourself or with one other player. There's no need to sit and fume because somebody who doesn't know better is holding you up.

- Do be a good sport, if for no other reason than because disc golf is a good sport.

- Do allow singles or doubles to play through when you're in a large, slow-moving group.

- Do always have fun!

SUMMARY

At the end of the day (or round), disc golf is only a game. Whether you're playing competitively against others or only against yourself, at all times extending common courtesy and using common sense is what best facilitates a good time for all. Even on the worst of days, there's no need to be a spoiler for those around you by being less than considerate of their enjoyment on the course.

It's a game, play it!

Chapter Ten
VARIATIONS OF THE GAME

Just as with many other sports, there are a number of game-play variations that can provide additional enjoyment and challenge to disc golf. In case you're so inclined, which I'm sure you will be, here are some of the most common variations.

PLAYING DOUBLES

Playing doubles is not only fun and often moves faster for groups of four and six, but also it is a great way to facilitate the development of new players' skills. Teams are paired off and play the course the traditional way with all rules intact, but with one big difference – only the best throw of each team is played.

For example, off the tee both members of each team drive, they then select which of their throws they wish to play next. At the agreed upon approach lie, both teammates take their next shot and then choose the best to use as they proceed. The throwing continues this way until one member of each team completes it with a successful putt.

New players get shot opportunities they don't normally get when playing on their own. This is particularly true when one teammate is a right hander and the other a southpaw. Since so many of our discs routinely fade to the opposite side of our throwing arm, a righty playing with a lefty will get access to unusual basket routes. Also, it allows players to try out new techniques they might otherwise be reluctant to experiment with; after all, their partner can always play the safe shot.

PLAYING UNMARKED COURSES

Not every disc golf course is lucky enough to have proper chain baskets. Some, in fact, have only iron poles or trees or wooden stakes or other objects to use as targets, but provide no clue as to where they are located. Figuring out the course layout can be nearly impossible without the guidance of someone already familiar with it. The lack of steel pin holes should not deflate your enjoyment of playing disc golf. In fact, although it can be a bit tough on the discs themselves, playing targets like trees can be pretty challenging. A target will be designated (perhaps a tree or pole), with a specific spot marked as the point below which the disc must strike in order to "hole out."

One nifty thing about courses like this, at least in the case where you really have no idea where you're going, is you can improvise and select challenging targets as you go. The more challenging the target is to reach, of course, the more fun it is to come up with throws to handle it. Trash bins, benches, scampering ferrets – almost anything can be a target!

Another cool thing to do is to improvise mandies (mandatories) for each hole.

PLAYING MANDIES ON THE FLY

Whether on a professionally maintained playing field or some unmarked non-basket course, one way to break up the monotony of throwing at the same old holes the same old way is to call mandies (mandatories) as you go along.

Whoever tees first calls the mandatory, although I think it's quite fun to have the player who tees off first have to perform the mandey selected by a player who tees next and wants the pad back. This definitely keeps the pressure on! A mandey call might be a specific area selected that the disc must travel either over, under or through, maybe even a combination of all three, which will be particularly challenging. Another mandey call could be a specific type of shot that must be used. For instance, the drive off this hole must be a helix out over the road and back into the ravine, or a roller across the field and over the ditch. The possibilities are endless, and the frustrations sometimes incalculable!

HOW TO PLAY ULTIMATE

While not really disc golf at all (because disc golf discs are not used) the game is appropriate to be included here.

Ultimate is increasingly popular and wildly fun. Where it inherently lacks all the majorly important Zen-like qualities of disc golf (see Chapter Twelve: The Zen of Disc Golf) it makes up for it in team participation, enthusiasm and challenge to your physical stamina. You see, ultimate is a high-energy coed team sport that requires lots and lots of running.

The way the game goes down is this: two teams consisting of seven players each, have at it on a playing field measuring 70 yards long by 40 yards wide. An end zone 25 yards deep is set up at opposing ends of the field. Players try to hurl the disc to their teammates in effort to do what essentially is like hockey or soccer. A player catches the disc, comes to an immediate standstill while usually being guarded by a member of the opposition's team, and has only ten seconds to throw it to another teammate. When a player catches a disc in their team's end zone - score! Lots of fun, this one.

HOW TO PLAY AROUND NINE

From the mind of Frisbee & disc golf pioneer "Steady" Ed Headrick comes this surprisingly enjoyable game, which can be played either indoors or outdoors. Geared for any number of players, it entails simply taking nine shots at a basket from fixed positions rotating around the basket at different distances (Figure 10.1).

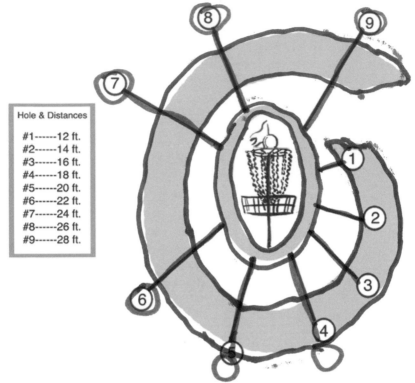

Hole & Distances	
#1	12 ft.
#2	14 ft.
#3	16 ft.
#4	18 ft.
#5	20 ft.
#6	22 ft.
#7	24 ft.
#8	26 ft.
#9	28 ft.

Figure 10.1 – Around Nine position chart.

The first throw is made from position one – also called the tee step or tee stone – twelve feet away from the basket. Make the putt, you get a point. Proceed to position two, which is rotated clockwise and two feet farther away from the basket, and take another shot. Sink the putt from there and you get two points. Continue along the positions, each one another two feet farther out, and if you make the shot, get points equal to its position. Sink all nine shots and guess what? You score 45 – a perfect game!

Sounds easy? Give it a try first, then let me know what you think!

SUMMARY

As you can see, there are all sorts of ways to increase your game playing fun through disc golf. I have no doubt that there are plenty more variations that exist than are listed here. Ask around, try out new ideas, even improvise with your mates and apply your own unique spin of the disc. Who knows, you just might create the next disc golf craze!

Chapter Eleven
THE ZEN OF DISC GOLF

There's a lot going on when playing disc golf. Whether in earnest competitive play against others or just against yourself, the game is as intense as you make it, and it's easy to make it intense on many different levels. Getting a good score is one level, certainly, but beyond the numbers lay other deeper, more profound and philosophical levels. For many players, disc golf is not unlike life itself. What with all the strolling around unhurriedly in the great outdoors, breathing in that fresh air and sopping up the good vibe surrounding you, every round affords ample opportunity for the enlightenment of truth, the universe and all things seriously significant.

That's why it's not uncommon to find your more contemplative players pontificating endlessly about important things of relevance and substance. Things such as, just how long can a pair of shorts be before they're actually considered pants?

Arguably, men's shorts become pants when they go past the mid-point of the calf. On women, shorts become pants at the top third of the calf. But if we accept this as truth the real question then becomes, where precisely is the calf's mid-point? And whose calf is it anyway? You see how heady it can get?

Yes, disc golf is life, and like life, it shares secrets only to those tossing the course to enlightenment. When you get right down to it, it's no mystery why disc golfers are thought to be right tossers!

That said, consider these words of wisdom for greater disc golf living:

THE DISC OF LIFE

The disc symbolizes your greatest possession, which is the potential of accomplishment. The disc is the vessel in which your dreams are contained, your energy invested, your future cast. Fling the disc without focus and you may find your life – without warning – spiralling unpredictably out of control. This is not necessarily a bad thing, for each unplanned lie can afford greater challenge with the prospect of immeasurable reward. But be warned, disc golfer, some lies hold truths we are unprepared to face.

All is in the disc and all-knowing it is.

BE THE BASKET

Resolute in its duty, outwardly the pin basket may appear steely cold while gleaming under the hot sun. Sentient guardian of that most coveted of awards (the "hole out"), it is immobile and uncompromising in its expectations of you, setting a very high standard. But look again, disc golfer. Are not the basket's chains like arms draped monkishly, awaiting only that precious moment to embrace you? Is it not patient in its effort to lift your spirit and validate your achievements? Does it not passively accept your treatment of it, even when you've been cruel and undeserving of such unconditional love?

This is the basket, your truest best friend. See the basket. Be the basket.

YOU'RE ALWAYS TREED UNTIL YOU'RE FREED

High is the disc perched in branches beyond your reach, though lofty is its intent. While the treed disc may seem to mock you, resisting mere mortal efforts to knock it to the earth, the disc is in fact urging you to reach higher than the limits you have, perhaps unknowingly, set for yourself. It is not so high as to be impossible to obtain.

As with the elusive disc gone irretrievably astray until spied in a tree, one is lost only until found by one's willingness to discover.

$#%! THIS HOLE

Like the road of life, the route to each hole is sometimes pitted by formidable obstacles. With each obstacle comes the prospect of challenges anew, the value of overcoming them determined only through the manner and mindset in which they are confronted. Go in with a bad attitude and too often you will emerge from the experience with a worse attitude. Seize the prospect of positive change through each challenge, no matter how many strokes it costs you.

The hole is empowering if you choose to make it so. Always remember, it's one toss at a time and one toss is all it takes.

THROW ONLY WHAT YOU'RE PREPARED TO CATCH UPSIDE THE HEAD

Life swirls unabated at all times around you, dear disc golfer. Be receptive to its presence. Inhale its simple splendors, and acknowledge them all with due respect and courtesy. For that which is recognized, as well as all unseen, are reminders that you, too, are a single, unprotected note in life's delicate harmony.

Honor the world with your intent so intent on you is the world. Otherwise you might get conked in the head by a disc!

HOLE ONE IS YOUR LAST

The manner in which one receives the day is determined the moment one elects how to embrace it. Even though sometimes veiled by dark clouds, the resuscitating reach of the sun still penetrates to infuse the earth with power. Whether winding up on the pad or slinging somewhere midway between it and the hole, the moment that matters is this ever-present one that is constantly changing, shaped only by the choices you make. Awareness of the moment is demonstrated through clarity of focus and intent, which can manifest itself in positive outcome regardless of what negative energy nudged you to the threshold of this moment on which you now stand.

Whatever the number assigned, there is no hole but the first which follows the last. Make of it what you choose.

THERE'S NO "PAR" IN A (W)HOLE

Wholeness is comprised of the lack of insubstantial. For lovers, one does not comprise a portion missing, but rather makes what is intanglbly incomplete a real and vibrant reminder of completeness when coupled with another. For disc golfers, what io rcol is the pursuit of the hole, each isolated unto itself to serve only your potential.

How long it takes to complete the hole is irrevelent. Without you, it is alone.

PLAY BECAUSE IT IS

One plays because such moments lend themselves to romping wildly without worry of reprisal — frolic for the sake of frivolity and nothing more. This moment, with the sky above and friends known and unmet around you, sharing the same dream, is the gift of fun. It exists to appreciate seriously, but not so seriously as to spoil the gift.

Wars are waged to win. Games are played to enjoy. You don't war in the sandbox.

Yes, disc golf is life. Might as well accept it going in and get used to it coming out!

Chapter 12
DISC GOLF RESOURCES

DISC MANUFACTURERS

CHING
Web site: www.chingpro.com

Discraft
Phone: 248-624-2250
Web site: www.discraft.com

Gateway
Phone: 314-429-3472
Web site: www.gatewaydiscsports.com

Innova
Phone: Innova West: 800-408-8449
Phone: Innova East: 800-476-3968
Web site: www.innovadiscs.com

Lightning
Phone: 214-328-9017
Web site: www.lightninggolfdiscs.com

Millenium
Web site: www.golfdisc.com

DISC GOLF-RELATED WEB SITES

There are so many places online offering merchandise, information, and helpful advice on improving your game that providing a comprehensive list would require a book devoted only to that. Here are only a few prime places to start.

DiscGolf.com (portal)
www.discgolf.com

DiscGolferUSA.com
www.discgolferusa.com

Disc Golf World
www.discgolfworld.com

Disc Life – Online Disc Golf Magazine
www.disclife.com

Gotta Go Throw
www.gottagogottathrow.com

Ken Climo (Eleven-time PDGA World Champion, three-time U.S. Open Champion)
www.kenclimo.com

Play Disc Golf
www.playdiscgolf.com

Scott Stokely (21-time World and National disc golf and distance champion)
www.scottstokely.com

Zingcrash
www.zingcrash.com

PROFESSIONAL DISC GOLF ASSOCIATION

PDGA
3841 Dogwood Lane
Appling, GA 30802-3004
Phone: 706-261-6342
Web site: www.pdga.com

DISC GOLF ASSOCIATION

DGA
16 Maher Road
Watsonville, CA 95076
Phone: 831-722-6037
Web site: www.discgolfassoc.com

DISC GOLF COURSE LOCATIONS

There are nearly 1400 disc golf courses in the world, with over 1100 located in the United States. The easiest way to locate the courses nearest you is by visiting the Professional Disc Golf Association's Web site at www.pdga.com and checking its searchable directory. You can even download a PDGA Course Directory to your Palm Pilot for free.

DISC GOLF GLOSSARY

Anhyzer - The angle of release that results in a disc fading to the direction of the player's throwng arm.

Approach Disc - A disc used primarily for shorter throws, usually on the fairway.

Approximate Lie - A lie established by the player's group in order to correct a misplay (a disc falling out-of-bounds, a lost disc, a disc mistakenly picked up by another player, etc.)

Away Player - The player whose lie is farthest from the hole and who will throw next.

Birdie - Scoring one stroke under par.

Bogey - Scoring one stroke over par.

Casual - A non-permanent hazard on the course, such as bodies of water from rain or a pile of cleared brush, etc.; also a reference to non-tournament players.

Chainstar - A brand name disc golfing target, or basket. Other brands include Pole Hole and DISCatcher.

Completion of a Round - In competition play, the round has been officially completed for all players when, in the director's opinion, the last group on the course has completed their final hole and has had reasonable time to walk from their final hole to tournament headquarters.

Director - The person in charge of a tournament.

Disc Entrapment Device - A target used to complete the hole, usually consisting of an upper entrapping section of chains, cables, tubes, etc. and a lower entrapping section of a basket or tray.

Disc Bag - A lightweight bag, usually with a shoulder strap, used to store discs and other essentials while playing.

DISCatcher - A brand name disc golfing target, or basket. Other brands include Pole Hole and Chainstar.

Drop Zone - An area on the course, as designated by the course designer or director, from which play is resumed after the preceding shot (1) was thrown out-of-bounds, (2) missed a mandatory, or (3) landed in a protected area.

Driver - A disc designed for fast, long-distance flight.

Double-Bogey - Holing out two throws over par.

Eagle - Holing out two throws under par.

Fade - The direction in which a disc falls as its rotation slows during flight.

Fairway - The in-bounds path or field over which a player throws while advancing from the teeing position to the hole.

Falling Putt - A putt after which a player touches his or her mini marker disc, or any object beyond the lie, including the playing surface, before having demonstrated full control of balance.

Frisbee - A trademark name for a product made by Wham-O, often confused for the distincly different discs designed specifically for disc golf play.

Group - In recreational play, those players who advance along the course together. In competition, players who are assigned to play a round together for the purpose of verifying scores and proper play in accordance with the tournament rules.

Hole - The target that must be reached in order to complete that segment of the course. The term "hole" also refers to the numbered segments of the course that are separate units for scoring.

Holed Out - A term used to signify completion of a hole. A player has "holed out" after the removal of the at rest disc from the chains or entrapment area of a disc entrapment device or after striking the marked area of the designated object target.

Hyzer - The angle of release that results in a disc fading to the opposite direction of the player's throwng arm.

Lie - The spot on the playing surface where a player's previous throw has landed (or been designated as a result of a misplay), upon which the thrower must take his or her stance to throw again.

Line of Play - The imaginary line on the playing surface extending from the center of the target through the center of the marker disc and beyond.

Mandatory, mandey or mando - A designated flight path that a disc must travel on its way to the hole.

Marker - A term used to indicate either the mini-marker disc or the thrown disc at rest, both of which can be used to indicate the lie from which a thrower's next shot should be played.

Marker Disc - See Marker.

Obstacle - Any feature of the course that may impede any aspect of play.

Official - A person who is authorized to make judgments regarding the proper application of the rules during play.

Out-of-Bounds - An area designated prior to the start of play from which a disc may not be played. The out-of-bounds line extends a plane vertically upward and downward. The out-of-bounds line is itself in bounds.

Overstable - A term used to describe a disc that tends to fade in the opposite direction of a player's throwing side when released flat.

Par - The number of throws an accomplished disc golfer is expected to make to complete a given hole.

Penalty Throw - A throw added to a player's score for violating a rule, or for relocation of a lie, as called for by a rule.

Pole Hole - A brand name disc golfing target, or basket. Other brands include Chainstar and DISCatcher.

Putt - Any throw from ten meters or less as measured from the rear of the marker disc to the base of the hole.

Putter - A disc designed for short throws at the basket.

Sandbagger - A tournament player who competes in a division below his or her skill level.

Stable - A term used to describe a disc that tends to fly generally straight when released flat, regardless of the player's throwing side.

Supporting Point - Any part of a player's body that is in contact with the playing surface or some other object capable of providing support, at the time of release.

Tail Skate - Term used to describe what results when a disc is released with its nose up, so that it is pushing air.

Taco - Term used for a warped disc.

Teeing Area - The area bounded by the edges of a tee pad (if provided); otherwise, the area extending three meters perpendicularly behind the designated tee line.

Overstable - A term used to describe a disc that tends to fade in the direction of a player's throwing side when released flat.

Unsafe Lie - A lie from which a player decides that obstacle make it impractical or unsafe in either stance or throwing motion to attempt a throw. The lie is relocated with a penalty.

Worm burner - A shot that is released at a downward angle, resulting in a premature landing.

Appendix A – DISC CHEAT SHEET

Disc	Range	Flights	Description
#1 Driver	Long to very long drives Longest driver for beginners	Straight shots Slight right curve	Stable driver when new Will "s" curve when older
#3 Driver	Long drives	Straight or slight right turn	Will turn right at high speeds Flies flat at medium speed
#3 Flyer (Spitfire)	Long to very long drives	Straight shots	Stable at high speed Overstable at low speeds
APX	Putter, driver	Short to medium range drives and putts	Great putter and driver Good for accuracy shots
Archangel	Long range driver	Straight	Understable at high speeds
Aviar	Putts, approach, short drives	Straight shot Good control disk	Stable putter, stable driver Also available in KC Pro plastic
Aviar – X JK Pro	Approach, medium drives	Medium drives	Overstable Aviar Floats good
Banshee	Long to very long drives	Good for long headwind shots	Fades hard left at slow speeds Available in DX and KC Pro plastic
Birdie	Putts, approach shots	Straight shots Good first putter	Slightly overstable putter
Blowfly	Putts, approach shots	Overstable flyer	Very sticky plastic, very thick rim Falls left at end of flight
Blunt Putt	Putts, approach shots, short right turn shots	Straight flying putt and approach disc	Thick rim feels good in your hand
Cheetah	Extremely long drives	Stable at high speeds Slight right curve	Good long distance for beginner Available in DX and KC Pro plastic
Classic Roc	Good midrange driver	Low profile with bead	Also good for upshots and putts
Cobra	Long to very long drives	Straight shots slight right curve	Stable drives
Comet	Medium long drives	Straight shots Holds all curves well	Classic Great disc to learn with
Cyclone	Super distance driver	Straight shots, left curves	Great overstable driver Great feeling plastic
Cyclone Fly Dye	Super distance driver	Slightly more overstable than the Cyclone	Psychedelic fly dye plastic
Cyclone 2	Super distance driver More overstable than Cyclone	Straight shots into a headwind, left curves	More overstable than Cyclone
Eagle	Very long drives	Hard left curves Great headwind disc	Overstable flyer that requires a lot of snap Available in DX, KC Pro and champion Edition plastic
Eclipse	Extremely long drives	Straight shot Falls hard left at low speed	Large diameter Stable at high speed Overstable at low speed
Firebird	Super overstable	Hard left curves Low profile windbeater	Flies straighter as it wears in

Firebird – Champion Edition	Very overstable drive	Hard left curves best for strong throwers	Champion Edition plastic is super durable – indistructable
Firebird – KC Pro Edition	Stable distance driver	Flies straight and far	KC Pro plastic
Flathead Cyclone	Distance driver	Cyclone with low dome, flies fast and straight	Less durable plastic
Gator	Most overstable midrange disc	Good for power throwers	Flies fast for midrange disc
Gazelle	Super long drives	Stable at high speed Overstable at low speed	This the driver that 10 time world champion Ken Climo drives with, 'nuff said' Available in DX and KC Pro plastic
JLS	Extremely long drives Longest flyer for average thrower	Stable long distance driver	Holds straight line at high speed Fades left at low speed
Leopard	Super distance driver	Turnover distance disc	Understable at medium high speeds Good first driver for beginner Available in DX, Special Edition and Champion Edition plastic
Magnet	Putter, approach, short shots	Straight shots Good control disc	Stable flying putter or short driver
Moray	Long to very long drives	Long straight shots	Straight shots except downwind Will fade slightly left
MRX	Midrange drives	Fast midrange driver Slightly overstable	Discraft Elite Pro plastic
Omega	Putts, approach, short drives	Straight shots Good control disc	Comes in three different types of material – super soft, soft, stiff
Panther	Medium drives	Stable drives and long range putter	Smooth edge and 21 cm makes this a great first disc
Piranha	Putts, approach shots	Straight shots	Stable putter
Polaris LS	Super long drives	Stable at high speed Overstable at low speed	One of the longest flyers on the market Durable and gripable Falls left at end of flight
Polecat	Putter, approach, short shots	Straight shots Good control disc	Stable flying putter or short range driver
Prostyle DI	Super distance driver	Understable at high speeds Overstable at low speeds	High grade plastic and has grip rings
Puma	Medium to long drives	Straight shots Falls left at low speed	Stable at high speed Overstable at low speed
Rattler	Putter, short shots	Slow moving putter Short approach disc	Stable putter at all speeds
Rhyno	Medium range driver, putter	Short to medium range Over stable drives and putts	Edge like an Aviar with lowered dome and thumb rail Available in DX plastic for drives and gumb plastic for putts

Roc	Medium to long drives	Very straight shots	Flies straight even into a headwind Available in DX, KC Pro and Special Edition plastic
Rubber putter	Puts/short to medium drives	Straight shots Slight left curves	Slightly overstable Floats in water
Shark	Long drives	Stable driver	All purpose driver
Spider	Midrange driver	Stable	Nice plastic
Stingray	Long to very long drives	Straight shots Slight right curves	Stable driver Good first driver
Stratus	Long to very long drives	Straight and right turns	Stable driver Will hold a right turn for a long time
Superglide XL	Distance driver	XL with low dome Flies fast and straight	Less durable plastic
T-bird	Long to very long drives	#1 driver for pros	Stable at high speeds Overstable at low speeds Available in DX, KC Pro and Champion Edition plastic
Upshot	Putts, approach shots	Straight shots Good first putter	Stable putter with grip rings on the under rim.
U-2 Putter	Putts/short to medium drives	Straight putts Soft grippy material	Stable putter, low profile Grip rings under rim
Valkyrie	Very low profile, very fast flyer Extreme long distance	Understable at high speeds Overstable at low speeds	Fastest flying disc and probably longest for average throwers
Valkyrie – SE	Extremely long distance, very fast flyer	Understable at high speeds Overstable at low speeds	Just like standard Valkyrie, but in grippy, more durable plastic
Valkyrie – Champion Edition	Extremely long distance, very fast flyer	Stable at high speeds, overstable at low speeds	Most durable plastic, to times more durable than standard plastic
Whippet	Very long drives Very fast	Super overstable driver Good into headwind	Best thrown nosed over to the right It will "s" back to the left at end of flight Available in DX and KC Pro plastic
X2	Very long drives	Very long distance Slight left curves	Stable at high speeds Slightly overstable as it slows down
X-Clone	Very long drives Very fast	Super overstable driver Good into headwind Great disc for sidearm throwers	Best thrown nosed over to the right It will "s" back to the left at end of flight
XD	Midrange drives	Flies straight at medium speeds Understable at high speeds	Good driver for average player to learn with
XL	Very long distance	Stable at high and medium speeds	Made of high durability plastic This baby's the real deal
XL – Fly dye	Very long distance	Slightly more overstable than the XL	Psychedelic fly dye plastic

X-Press	Long distance	Understable at high speeds	Good distance driver for average player who has trouble with discs hyzering out too early
XS	Extremely long distance Holds world's distance record	Understable at high speeds Overstable at low speeds	Discraft Elite Pro plastic New world distance
ZXS	Extremely long distance	Stable at high speeds Overstable at low speeds	Discraft's super durable plastic with see through dome
ZXL	Extremely long distance	Moderately over stable	Ultra-durable, hooks left
Z Express	Discraft's longest flyer for new players	Stable	Ultra-durable Hooks left
Z Reaper	Extremely long flyer	Stable at high speeds Overstable at low speeds	Ultra-durable Hooks left

Courtesy of Morley Field Disc Golf Course, San Diego, CA.

Index

Trellis Publishing, Inc.
DIRECT ORDER FORM
Disc Golf: All You Need to Know about the Game You Want to Play

- Fax orders: 218-722-3194
- Telephone orders: Call Toll Free: 1 (800) 513-0115.
- Postal orders: Trellis Publishing, Inc.
  P.O. Box 16141
  Duluth, MN 55816

Bill and Ship to:
Company Name: _____
Contact Person: _____
Address:_____
City: _____ State: _____ Zip: _____-_____
Daytime telephone: (_____) _____ e-mail_____

Ordering Information

	Retail	Quantity	Price	Total
Disc Golf	$9.95	_____	_____	_____
			Subtotal:	_____

Quantity Discounts:

Quantity	Discount	Price
3-4	20%	$7.95
5-24	40%	$5.95
25 or more	50%	$4.95

Shipping:		
$1.00 - $20	$ 3.00	
$20.01- $40	$ 4.00	
$40.01- $70	$ 6.00	
$70.01- $120	$ 8.00	
$120.01-$200	$12.00	
Over $200	6% of order	_____

(Minnesota Residents add 6.5% tax) _____

Total Price: _____

Type of Payment:
____ Cheque enclosed, Payable to: Trellis Publishing, Inc.
____ Credit Card: ☐VISA ☐MASTERCARD ☐AMERICAN EXPRESS

Card number_____
Name on card: _____ Expiration Date: _____ /_____
Signature:_____